On the Arbitrary Nature of Things

On the Arbitrary Nature of Things

——— An Agnostic Reading of Hegel's *Phenomenology of Spirit* ———

Andrew Lee Bridges

☙PICKWICK *Publications* • Eugene, Oregon

ON THE ARBITRARY NATURE OF THINGS
An Agnostic Reading of Hegel's *Phenomenology of Spirit*

Copyright © 2022 Andrew Lee Bridges. All rights reserved. Except for brief quotations in critical publications or reviews, no part of this book may be reproduced in any manner without prior written permission from the publisher. Write: Permissions, Wipf and Stock Publishers, 199 W. 8th Ave., Suite 3, Eugene, OR 97401.

Pickwick Publications
An Imprint of Wipf and Stock Publishers
199 W. 8th Ave., Suite 3
Eugene, OR 97401

www.wipfandstock.com

PAPERBACK ISBN: 978-1-6667-1405-0
HARDCOVER ISBN: 978-1-6667-1406-7
EBOOK ISBN: 978-1-6667-1407-4

Cataloguing-in-Publication data:

Names: Bridges, Andrew Lee, author.

Title: On the arbitrary nature of things : an agnostic reading of Hegel's *Phenomenology of Spirit* / by Andrew Lee Bridges.

Description: Eugene, OR : Pickwick Publications, 2022 | Includes bibliographical references.

Identifiers: ISBN 978-1-6667-1405-0 (paperback) | ISBN 978-1-6667-1406-7 (hardcover) | ISBN 978-1-6667-1407-4 (ebook)

Subjects: LCSH: Hegel, Georg Wilhelm Friedrich, 1770–1831. Phänomenologie des Geistes.

Classification: B2929 .B74 2022 (print) | B2929 .B74 (ebook)

04/08/22

Contents

Introduction | 1

Chapter 1: The Universal, the Arbitrary, and the Topsy-Turvy: Remaining Agnostic Given Hegel's *Phenomenology of Spirit* and Coherence Epistemologies | 20

Chapter 2: Reason, Phrenology, and Coherence Epistemologies | 50

Chapter 3: The Potentiality of Both the Divine Mind and the Arbitrary Particular (Human) Mind to Become Universalized | 83

Chapter 4: Parting Company with Hegel after an Examination of Three Skeptical Discoveries: An Examination of "Religion in the Form of Art" | 108

Chapter 5: Examining the Cogency of Indistinguishability through the Phenomena of Sensoriums and the Placebo Effect | 133

Appendix A: Some Reflection on the Meaning of "Nature" | 163

Bibliography | 165

Introduction

Three Points of Skepticism in Hegel's
Phenomenology of Spirit

WHEN COMMENTING ON GREAT philosophers a critical distinction is often overlooked in the commentator's thoughts concerning the philosopher. This distinction is between the totality of what the philosopher said (either in a particular work or given all their works) and what the philosopher said which is most helpful or most interesting to later philosophers. Such amalgamations of these two very distinct purposes behind comments is nowhere more evident than in Hegel scholarship. Commentaries are often so intermingled in this respect that what I am attempting to clarify may still be nebulous when considering Hegel's work. Therefore, before we do so let me provide an example of what I mean to distinguish by utilizing another philosopher; a philosopher that when compared to Hegel, we might even call him a philosopher with a "more simple philosophy." Descartes is the philosopher who I have in mind to elucidate this distinction in philosophical commentary concerning great philosophers. So let us elucidate this distinction using Descartes' philosophy as an example before we move on to Hegel.

What I will now say about Descartes' work can be understood by and large as my own subjective opinion concerning the merit of Descartes philosophy. You, reading this, may hold a very different opinion on the matter—and I do not wish to debate the matter, but rather only to distinguish in kind the particular type of debate we would have if we did decided to debate the matter, from a very different type of debate commentators on great philosophers have. I draw this distinction not to enter into debate, but to elucidate the fact that the two debates (whatever one's opinions in the matter are) are quite different and that it is often unfortunate and confusing when these two separate debates amalgamate unintentionally. So, without further explanation, here is what I think about the merit of Descartes' philosophy: It is evident when reading Descartes' *Meditations on First Philosophy* that not every meditation is equally helpful or interesting to philosophers who follow. Introductory textbooks to the subject of philosophy often include excerpts from Descartes' *Meditations on First Philosophy*, but these texts know (in my opinion) not to include anything past the second meditation, because little past the second meditation is helpful for students being introduced to the subject of philosophy. If students, as they are being introduced to philosophy read the remaining four meditations they might think epistemological problems in philosophy are not as serious as they in fact are—but more than that: including the last four meditations of Descartes, in an introductory philosophy textbooks (as opposed to a Modern Philosophy Reader or a History of Philosophy text) may even do Descartes a disservice because the last four meditations take away from the philosophical merit of the first two meditations by suggesting that the solution to such profound skepticism can be found in the latter four meditations.

Do we now see the distinction between the totality of what a philosopher said, and what a philosopher said that is most helpful or most interesting to later philosophers? Obviously, the matters in debate may never be solved satisfactorily—that is not my intent. My intent is merely to elucidate the distinction between these two debates. With respect to the totality of what Descartes is saying in the *Meditations*, I find he is demonstrating that he is in possession of ontological proofs of the existence of God that alleviate skepticism and elucidate substance dualism. With respect to what Descartes is saying in the *Meditations* that is most helpful and most interesting to later philosophers, I find this to be that we have many reasons to be skeptical of almost everything except that we are thinking—now can we (as philosophers) think of any way to alleviate such skeptical worries? As part of the process of drawing this distinction, I want to take a moment to acknowledge that what I think is most helpful and most interesting about Descartes' philosophy can be best expressed in a view that Descartes himself does not endorse. Scholars may disagree with both how I have summarized the totality of Descartes thoughts concerning his *Meditations*, as well as with how I have summarized and selected what is useful and interesting in the *Meditations* for later philosophers, and they may even disagree with the merit of reading all

INTRODUCTION

of Descartes' *Meditations* in an introduction to philosophy class—and that's quite all right; my aim is not to argue the details of either of these points, but only to elucidate the distinction between them, that is, to explain that these two points are quite different indeed. With this distinction in mind between the totality of what a philosopher said, and what a philosopher said that is most helpful and most interesting to later philosophers, let us turn to Hegel's work, the *Phenomenology of Spirit*.

With respect to the *Phenomenology of Spirit* I suggest that there are three discoveries which Hegel makes that are his most helpful and interesting contribution to later philosophers, and that, much like with the example of Descartes' *Meditations*, the totality of what Hegel said in the *Phenomenology of Spirit*, actually takes away from the profundity of these three discoveries. The first discovery comes at the end of the section entitled "Force and the Understanding," during Hegel's topsy-turvy world philosophical thought-experiment, in which he ridicules the Kantian phenomena/noumena distinction. This discovery, which seems to be evident, though never explicitly stated by Hegel, I argue, is that what is universal and what is arbitrary need never contradict—and this discovery Hegel never seeks to resolve directly. The second discovery relates thoroughly to the chapters of "Reason" and "Spirit." In these chapters, Hegel, unlike any philosopher before him, understands that variety in customs and habit influence inductive reasoning in various ways, such that any two things might seem to be connected causally in a particular form of reasoning of a particular people at a particular time. Hume, of course, suggested this possibility with the problem of induction, and its unsatisfactory justification being found ultimately in custom and habit, but Hegel provides such a rich variety of absurd forms of reasoning so as to make the reader think that given the right customs and habits, a person could confidently believe anything. This is the second equally alarming discovery that Hegel makes in the *Phenomenology of Spirit* which is of great interest to philosophers after Hegel. This second skeptical discovery is that coherence epistemologies allow the absurd ("the absurd" is only considered absurd to those who do not subscribe to the particular epistemology) to become a historical reality, in which Hegel sees Phrenology as a prime example.

The third discovery which Hegel makes is the idea that if aspects of history are told in a way that appears to rationally justify particular customs and habits, and they reinforce a particular form of inductive reasoning, then the customs and habits seem not only rational but natural, and are actualizable in both ethical life and religious communities. Put another way, this third discovery suggest a way in which a mind can be formed or adopted within particular social or cultural contexts via custom and habit. The suggestion of adopting a mind other than one's own is not an idea that is unfamiliar to Hegel, since he is familiar with the Christian tradition. We need only remember the suggestion the Apostle Paul makes to the Philippian Church immediately prior to the famous Philippians' Hymn, "Let this mind be in you, which was also in Christ Jesus." We wonder how a community can adopt a shared mind, regardless of whether the claim is that such a mind is divine or human, and Hegel provides alarming insights into possible answers to such a question, as early as the master-slave dialectic. Hegel, throughout the *Phenomenology*, acts more like a reporter, presenting the developments of Spirit in the field of time—supplying the reader with a profound reflection of Spirit's history—and not as a creator putting his own spin on historical events for his own purpose (i.e., Voegelin's criticism of Hegel's imaginative history).[1] Hegel presents Spirit as something real, which guides history and allows absolute knowing for those which comprehend its work in history—but the discovery which is most relevant for later philosophers, I argue, is to what extent supplying profound reflection on history, which serves to justify particular customs and habits, can essentially shape the mind of another person, regardless of if such a thing like Spirit exists. To borrow the language of the Apostle Paul, "Let this mind be in you, which was also in Hegel"—after the creation of the *Phenomenology of Spirit*, philosophy discovers the awareness of such a possibility, and that such a possibility could also be secular in nature.

Throughout this book I use the phrase "the indistinguishability between the arbitrary and the non-arbitrary nature of things." Let me first clarify what I mean by this phrase and, why I select these words to express my ideas, and to what extent the context of skepticism relates to this phrase and to the agnosticism it provokes. Let me also state that the epistemological position I find to be the most helpful and interesting result of the *Phenomenology* (though not a position that Hegel, himself, endorses) is not skepticism, relativism, or anti-realism—though it is similar to these positions in certain respects that will become evident as the description unfolds. The epistemological situation and the clarification of my terminology is

---

1. Furthermore, Voegelin writes "Hegel's choice of an imaginary absolute pole was 'Empire', understood as the ecumenic organization of mankind under the Idea in history; and the deformation of the cognitive core imposed the deformed style of cognition which produced the imaginary history of the Idea." Voegelin, "On Hegel," 426–37.

best reached by way of analogy: Imagine you are participating in a placebo test trial. You are given a substance. What is your epistemological attitude toward the nature of this substance? Your epistemological attitude cannot be described with complete accuracy as the position of skepticism, though there are skeptical elements contained in your epistemological attitude. I describe the epistemological situation in which a participant of the placebo test trial places you in—and therefore your epistemological description of the nature of the substance you are given—as, "the indistinguishability between the arbitrary and non-arbitrary nature of the thing." Your epistemological position is not skepticism, but rather agnosticism concerning the nature of this thing (this substance or treatment you are given). Its nature could be arbitrary; its nature could be non-arbitrary—you simply do not know. To further clarify my choice of terminology, "arbitrary and non-arbitrary" can be generally understood as being synonymous with "inessential and essential," but I prefer the former terminology because as I examine Hegel's critique of various forms of epistemology (such as sense certainty, perception, and understanding) "inessential and essential," take on slightly different meanings, which I find has the potential to inhibit overall clarity. It is for this reason that I have selected the terminology of "arbitrary and non-arbitrary." Now, without further hesitation, I will state the general thesis this book intends to demonstrate.

I intend to demonstrate that when the philosopher contemplates the three skeptical discoveries which the *Phenomenology of Spirit* brings to philosophers after Hegel, one finds an indistinguishability between the arbitrary and non-arbitrary nature of things. Here, let me remind us of the initial critical distinction I made at the beginning between the totality of what a philosopher said, and what a philosopher said that is most helpful or most interesting to later philosophers. I am in no way claiming that Hegel, himself, saw things as having arbitrary natures or that he thought of history unfolding in arbitrary ways—in fact he repeatedly states just the opposite throughout his work. What I am saying however is, much like the case of Descartes' *Meditations*, I find the skeptical worries which Hegel creates in his work are of much greater import than the solutions he provides, which at the end of the day leaves philosophy with greater skepticism than it once had before the work was created. But this is not to say that after one reads the *Phenomenology* one finds that skepticism is ones only recourse—rather I argue that agnosticism most accurately captures the epistemological position one is in after, on the one hand, being provided a path to absolute knowing and on the other hand being confronted by the three aforementioned skeptical discoveries. In the following chapters I aim to elucidate each of these three discoveries within the *Phenomenology* and then show the skepticism each discovery brings. After devoting a chapter to each one of these points of skepticism, I spend the fourth chapter explaining how the compound effects of these three skeptical worries leads to the conclusion that there is an indistinguishability between the arbitrary and non-arbitrary nature of things. Lastly I look at two phenomena in our contemporary context—the placebo effect and the integration of sensoriums into phenomenological anthropology—as a way of exploring the credence behind the skepticism which leads to the conclusion that there is an indistinguishability between the arbitrary and non-arbitrary nature of things.

Skeptical Developments concerning Hegel's *Phenomenology*

Although there have been individuals skeptical of Hegel's task and intentions concerning his aims in the *Phenomenology of Spirit*, such as Voegelin, there has yet to be a comprehensive work dedicated to the manifold epistemological skepticism that results from the *Phenomenology of Spirit*. It is the aim of the current work to supply the groundwork for such a work. To this end, in this section I will focus on the literature that suggest sections of the *Phenomenology of Spirit* address particularly forms of skepticism and therefore criticize particular types of epistemologies. The first point to be addressed will concern the section entitled "Force and Understanding," as well as some of the material from the prior section involving epistemological questions concerning perception. The second point to be addressed will concern "Observing Reason," and the epistemological criticism and limitation of such reasoning with particular focus on Phrenology. Lastly, the skepticism of Hegel's aim in general, i.e., absolute knowing will be explored, with attention given to any literature that may provide insight into our epistemological situation after Hegel's *Phenomenology of Spirit*, particularly, if the certainty of Hegel's epistemological goals are not shared by his wider philosophical audience whereas his critique of epistemology is.

Concerning the section of the *Phenomenology of Spirit* entitled "Force and Understanding," commentators are divided on the issue concerning how the topsy-turvy world relates to Force and Understanding, and then by implication, how this relation, itself, relates to comprehending how

INTRODUCTION

Hegel is directing the thoughts of his readership to move from consciousness to self-consciousness. The analysis of this section in which the current work focuses on most for the epistemological uncertainties that it suggests is in an essay entitled, "Hegel's *Phenomenology of Spirit*," by Robert Solomon as well as some of Solomon's other works. In this essay, Solomon explains that "while the chapter called 'Force and understanding' is essentially Kantian, it contains a powerful critique of Kant's *Critique* and suggests that the laws of nature are not merely imposed but inherent in the world itself. In other words, Hegel rejects the Kantian insistence that we should not look for 'the universal laws of nature in nature' but rather 'in the conditions of possibility of experience.'"[2]

The article goes on to explain that "the inverted-world passage is essentially an argument by ridicule, for what becomes evident is that, if we take Kant's notion of noumenon seriously, any sort of nonsense becomes equally intelligible. Either the noumenal world is just like the phenomenal world, or, not only does it not make sense to talk about it, but it does not even make sense to suppose that there might be one."[3] This particular explanation by Solomon aims to elucidate particular passages concerning the topsy-turvy world such as the following: "This means that what in the law of the first world is sweet, in this inverted in-itself is sour, what in the former is black is, in the other, white."[4] In this explanation, the topsy-turvy world relates to the Kantian notion of the Understanding (as well as to Kant's transcendentalism, generally), and it is meant to ridicule such Understanding by addressing the epistemological limitations of not having access to the Noumenal world—not having access to the infinite. For Solomon, the topsy-turvy world acts as a philosophical thought-experiment that provides the reader with an argument for rejecting Kantian epistemology, and a willingness to reconceive the way in which the finite and the infinite are related.[5]

2. Solomon, "Hegel's *Phenomenology of Spirit*," 198.
3. Solomon, "Hegel's *Phenomenology of Spirit*," 200.
4. Hegel, *Phenomenology Of Spirit*, 97.
5. Hegel's notion of infinity seeks to resolve this distinction by claiming that infinity is the unity of opposites and is found both in the Notion and in the object. Hegel's view of infinity is nuanced in this way because, as Michael Inwood correctly points out, Hegel observes two problems with conventional understandings of infinity. Inwood articulates the first problem Hegel finds with this traditional understanding of infinity by explaining that "if the infinite is distinct from the finite, it is limited by the finite and is thus finite rather than infinite." The second problem Inwood states by explaining that for Hegel, "an infinite regress or an infinite progress(ion) is vicious intellectually incoherent and practically self-defeating." The primary application for Hegel's nuanced notion of infinity

This view of Solomon's is described as well in two of his other works; in *In the Spirit of Hegel*, he explains that "in the inverted world, sweet things are sour and pleasure is pain. Reward is punishment, and law is crime. Taken literally, this is nonsense, but that is just what it is intended to be, for this is a *reduction ad absurdum* argument against any notion of a supersensible world; if it is the same as the sensible world, we don't need it."[6] Furthermore, in *From Hegel to Existentialism*, Solomon writes, "In a perplexing but delightful counterexample of sorts, Hegel creates an 'inverted' (*verkehrte*) supersensible world, in which it is suggested that every proposition true of the apparent world corresponds to its *opposite* in the 'real' world (black is white, good is evil). And so, Hegel rejects, by making fun of, Kant's 'things-in-themselves' as distinct from phenomena."[7]

This view of the topsy-turvy world appears to have originated in the work of Joseph C. Flay, in particular in this article entitled, "Hegel's 'Inverted World.'" In this work Flay describes an aim to supplement (as opposed to disagree with) other interpretations of this section of the *Phenomenology of Spirit*—interpretations such as those of Hyppolite and Gadamer. Flay begins this paper by suggesting "that this 'inverted world' is exactly that: an absurd position. This is not to say that it is to be ignored or condemned as 'fantastic,' but rather that its importance and intelligibility lay in its very absurdity, in its *appearance* as an unintelligible inversion of what previously was taken to constitute the intelligibility of the world of appearance."[8] Flay then suggests that the context in which such intelligibility of "the world of appearance," should be considered with respect to the inverted world, is the prior context of the former systems of Kant and Leibniz.

No literature I have found, however, explores the possibility that Hegel is effective in devastating the Kantian epistemological position, but

---

is that Geist (i.e., God as immanent in the world) is not distinct from the world, nor from history. The various forms of consciousness presented in the imaginative history of Hegel's *Phenomenology* are the appearances of Geist mediated by the historical situation in which they appear. Inwood, *A Hegel Dictionary*, 140.

6. When discussing the interpretation of the supersensible world, Solomon maintains that two different answers to its relevance might be more thorough than any one perspective. Here he explains that "Two suggestions have been prominent in the literature; one is the idea that the inverted world offers us an intentionally ridiculous counter-example to Kant's notion of the 'thing-in-itself.' The other suggestion is that the inverted world actually makes the point that the real world is itself contradictory. I now think that a better interpretation includes both of these." Solomon, *In the Spirit of Hegel*, 380–81.

7. Solomon, *From Hegel to Existentialism*, 21.

8. Flay, "Hegel's 'Inverted World,'" 662.

INTRODUCTION

ineffective in providing his reader with absolute knowing in the context of the infinite, and therefore the end result is skepticism (or agnosticism) concerning the nature of things. It is the aim of the current work to further explore this possibility, and in particular to explore the idea that the reason why the topsy-turvy world thought-experiment is so devastating to Kantian epistemology, is that the possibility that what is universal and what is arbitrary need not ever contradict—and that such a possibility is to a certain extent encouraged (epistemologically) in the Kantian system because Kant looks for universal laws of nature in the conditions of the possibility of experience as opposed to looking for such laws in nature. The work "Truth and Self-Satisfaction," by Robert Solomon, comes closest to approaching this particular question in a few ways. It does so first by connecting the topsy-turvy world philosophical thought-experiment— which again it explains to be a critique of the Kantian phenomena/noumena distinction—to a critique of coherence epistemologies.[9] Second the article does so by exploring the inadequacies of epistemology (correspondence, coherence, and pragmatic) to confidently determine the nature of a thing, after Hegel's critique of epistemologies (ways of knowing such as sense-certainty, perception, and understanding) in the *Phenomenology of Spirit*.[10] The article stresses that though each epistemological approach

9. Here Solomon explains, "A frequent objection to the coherence theory is the following: any system of coherent beliefs can be turned into an equally coherent system by the systematic application of some logical operator, e.g., by turning each belief into its contradictory. That is, there might be equally coherent but mutually incompatible systems of belief, and it would not seem to make sense to say that they are both equally 'true.' This argument has its clear instantiation in the *Phenomenology*. Hegel offers us the absurd counter-example of a '*Verkehrte*' or 'inverted' world, in which black is white, light is heavy, good is evil, and so on. His ultimate target is Kant's distinction between noumenon and phenomenon, but the example holds as well against coherence theory. It is a material equivalence of the replacement of each true proposition with its contradictory, and the result is absurd. Truth cannot be mere coherence. But neither, Hegel argues, can truth be divorced from our beliefs, from the categories or our 'forms of consciousness.' If mere coherence is *not enough* for truth, the Kantian insistence that our beliefs correspond to the world as it is independently of us is *too much*, for an adequate notion of truth." Solomon, "Truth and Self-Satisfaction," 704.

10. Here Solomon explains, "How is it that there are 'facts'? Or, in Nineteenth Century terminology, what is 'determination' or 'constitution' of the facts? The Kantian-Hegelian reply charges our imaginations, but is ultimately equivocal. The metaphor is typically one of 'giving form to,' and the tool of the metaphor is 'the concept' or, what is the same thing, 'rules of the understanding.' But it is never clear, in Kant, Fichte, or Hegel, to what extent this means *creation* and to what extent it means only *interpretation*." (In the current work, I articulate this aforementioned ambiguity as the indistinguishability

9

has explanatory merit, part of the inadequacy of each lies in the fact that they do not appear to fully explain how one is to understand the merits of the other two types of epistemology. Solomon suggests that Hegel's approach does attempt to satisfy his reader by acknowledging the merits behind different ways of knowing.

With respect to how one should apprehend Hegel's treatment of phrenology and its connection to the topsy-turvy world and to skepticism, the literature on the matter finds the two subjects related both directly and indirectly. Phrenology relates directly to the topsy-turvy world and to skepticism in the work *Hegel's Recollection: A Study of Images in the Phenomenology of Spirit,* by Donald Phillip Verene. In this work, Verene dedicates a chapter to Phrenology in which he explains, "Phrenology is the inverted world, the upside-down version of phenomenology.... Phrenology must be attacked so strongly, as an illusion of consciousness in its road to self-knowledge, not simply because it is pseudo-science and representing bad thinking, but because it is the natural opposite, the inversion of the true science of mind—phenomenology."[11] Verene likewise makes a similar association between Physiognomy and the topsy-turvy world; when comparing Physiognomy with the behaviorism of B. F. Skinner, Verene writes, "What can Skinner tell us of the psychopath who always wears the mask of sanity? With the question of the face as mask this science encounters the principle of the topsy-turvy world that consciousness experienced in its first attempt at understanding the object, at the end of the section on Consciousness (A). There consciousness faced the problem in terms of the inner and the outer of the object. Here it faces it in terms of the inner and outer of the subject. Hegel says: "Observation accepts this antithesis in the same inverted relationship which characterizes it in the sphere of appearance."[12] Here Verene appears to be suggesting that pseudosciences such as Phrenology and

---

between the arbitrary and non-arbitrary nature of things). Solomon goes on to say, "It is not as if our experiences in general follows the model of our 'constituting' the shape of a buxom woman in a grey mass of threatening cumulus clouds, or Camus' prisoner trying to 'constitute' the head of Christ in the shadows of his stucco cell wall. This dramatic model of epistemic creativity appears to leave out what many philosophers, e.g. Locke, have seen as a 'natural' and uncreative association between our ideas and our words and the matters which they 'represent.' One is reminded of the childhood joke, in which Eve calls out to Adam, 'Let's call that one a hippopotamus.' 'Why?' 'Well, because it certainly looks more like a hippopotamus than anything else we've seen so far.'" Solomon, "Truth and Self-Satisfaction," 714.

11. Verene, *Hegel's Recollection*, 89.
12. Verene, *Hegel's Recollection*, 84.

INTRODUCTION

Physiognomy are examples or manifestations of this idea of a topsy-turvy world, in which phenomenology serves to correct the absurd view which is present in history at a particular moment.

Phrenology relates indirectly to the topsy-turvy world thought-experiment when one questions whether this form of consciousness is to be understood as existing within a coherence epistemology (A position that the current work will argue for). Alasdair MacIntyre, for example, in his article entitled "Hegel on Faces and Skulls," makes comparisons between the assumptions of phrenology and neurophysiology,[13] and Verene, in his work *Hegel's Recollection: A Study of Images in the Phenomenology of Spirit* stresses the prevalence of phrenology during the time of Hegel,[14] and frequently compares phrenology to the behaviorism of B. F. Skinner. The current work explores the indirect association between phrenology and the topsy-turvy world—that indirect association being their mutual connection to coherence epistemologies. This is done by arguing Hegel shows concrete examples of the topsy-turvy world, such as phrenology, can come into existence in the real world through coherence epistemologies, and that this is but another

---

13. Here MacIntyre explains, "There is finally the thesis that the local activity of the brain is the sufficient cause and explanation of behavior, and that therefore the shape of the cranium allows us to predict behavior. Buried in these dubious contentions is one that is less obviously dubious, that is indeed familiar and widely accepted. I mean of course the thesis that there are biochemical or neural states of affairs, processes, and events, the occurrence and the nature of which are the sufficient causes of human actions. This thesis wore phrenological clothing in 1807; today its clothing is as fashionable as it was then, only the fashions are not what they were. Moreover, when Hegel attempted to rebut the claims of physiognomy and phrenology, he did so in such a way that if his rebuttal is successful it would hold against the thesis that I have just stated whatever its scientific clothing." MacIntyre, "Hegel on Faces and Skulls," 224–25.

14. Here Verene explains, "One might be tempted to say that there must be some difference between Skinner and such exponents of pseudo-science. Skinner is a controversial but respected figure in the profession of psychology. This is to forget that both Lavater and Gall were quite famous. Gall was a favorite of European aristocracy. Metternich the Austrian prince and statesman, thought him the greatest mind he had ever known; after his death Gall was mourned as a great pioneer scientist. Why would a science of lineaments be so attractive? Why is it so easily accepted? What accounts for the fact that this attitude of consciousness keeps coming back to us under various names, and will continue to do so, since it is a fundamental way in which consciousness relates to itself? Hegel's answer is that it is grounded in a sense of the individual's character that serves us every day in our intercourse with others. He says: 'We see from a man's face whether he is *in earnest* about what he is saying or doing' (Miller, 318). But the science of physiognomy, Hegel says, overlooks the power of the mask (ibid.). Skinner has overlooked this, too (of course he believes nothing can hide from the searchlight of scientific experimentation, consciously or unconsciously)." Verene, *Hegel's Recollection*, 84.

way that the topsy-turvy philosophical thought-experiment is not only a critique of the Kantian phenomena/noumena distinction, but also a critique of coherence epistemologies—a critique that results in agnosticism toward the knowledge coherence epistemologies make possible.

There is a direct link in the literature between Hegel's use of the topsy-turvy world thought-experiment and Hegel's criticism of Phrenology, as well as a direct link between Hegel's use of the topsy-turvy world and his critique of coherence epistemologies. There is also an indirect link between Phrenology and coherence epistemologies, with the question of whether Phrenology is best understood to exist within a coherence epistemology. Given that Verene compares Phrenology to the inversion of Phenomenology, the remaining point to consider, we assert, is whether commentators have understood the epistemology of Hegel's *Phenomenology of Spirit* to be best understood to rely on a coherence epistemology as well.

Richard Dien Winfield, in his article entitled, "Hegel versus the New Orthodoxy," describes both what the New Orthodoxy understands to be the self-defeating aspects of Hegel's own theory, as well as shares a critique of coherence epistemologies, which serves as a critique of naturalized epistemology as understood by the New Orthodoxy. Concerning the former, Winfield writes, "What the new orthodoxy finds so noteworthy in Hegel's account are the exhaustiveness and concreteness of its gallery of different foundational projects. Its exhaustiveness suggests that there can be no shape of knowing that does not operate in terms of a self-defeating appeal to givens. Hegel may claim to have reached a final shape of consciousness whose knowing is absolute. Nonetheless, so long as such knowing measures its knowledge against any putative given . . . the new orthodoxy has good reason to regard 'absolute knowing' as a misnomer, designating but one more shape of corrigible cognition."[15] Concerning the latter epistemological skepticism, which appears to inadvertently arise from the *Phenomenology of Spirit*, and to which the new orthodoxy itself is not immune, Winfield explains, "If, however, as the new orthodoxy claims, the phenomenological analysis of spirit shows how historical practices frame the givens and modes of reference by which knowledge claims are adjudicated, it is impossible for any historical formation to engender an absolute standpoint in which knowing is freed of the limits of representation. So long as given practices provide knowing with the foundations determining what it accepts as valid, every historical epoch and every frame of reference

---

15. Winfield, "Hegel versus the New Orthodoxy," 221.

INTRODUCTION

is equally tainted. Hence, Hegel's critique of epistemology undermines his own claims of wisdom, leaving behind the naturalized epistemology that transforms philosophy into edifying deconstruction."[16] Winfield however, voices concern that the critique of epistemology which the *Phenomenology of Spirit* ultimately provides, does not support the conclusion that naturalized epistemology possesses any validity as an alternative to Hegel's conclusion—and that the result is ultimately skepticism or uncertainty, of any claims naturalized epistemologies would make. This is most evident when Winfield claims, "If it [the new orthodoxy] seeks to escape this contradiction by regarding its own theoretical claims as burdened by foundational assumptions rooted in the practices of time, it must admit that its naturalized epistemology has no more authority than any other competing picture."[17] The current work explores the implications of such skepticism as a result of Hegel's *Phenomenology of Spirit*, with particular focus on the idea that from the topsy-turvy world thought-experiment, we are able to conclude that what is arbitrary and what is universal are compatible, and that what allows for such compatibility are coherence epistemologies, in which Phrenology is just one example which Hegel provides. We explore such implication in conjunction with the idea that Hegel's critique of coherence epistemologies applies to all systems of knowledge, including naturalized epistemologies, and including Hegel's own system.

Methodological Relationship between Skepticism and Agnosticism

My method for this agnostic reading of Hegel's *Phenomenology* is first to examine the chapters in the *Phenomenology of Spirit* in which such skeptical discoveries are developed. With respect to the first skeptical discovery I examine Hegel's topsy-turvy philosophical thought-experiment, and demonstrate that a result of this thought-experiment is that there exists the possibility for what is arbitrary and what is universal to be compatible. In a similar fashion, with respect to the second skeptical discovery, I examine Hegel's presentation on "Observing Reason," and in particular I examine how Hegel sees informal fallacies of inductive reasoning persisting in patterns of reasoning such as physiognomy, phrenology, and palmistry. In my examination of "Observing Reason," I argue that

16. Winfield, "Hegel versus the New Orthodoxy," 221.
17. Winfield, "Hegel versus the New Orthodoxy," 222.

Hegel has demonstrated that systems of reasoning can exists which have no accountability to actuality—and that they are able to persist because custom and habit do not allow arbitrary associations between two things or events—which are understood in a system of rationality to have a cause and effect relationship—to be proven falsifiable.

There are two aspects of Hegel's methodology which I find questionable: (1) That Hegel's readership find his presentation of Spirit's movement or work through history compelling, and that, therefore, by working through the movements of Spirit that Hegel describes, one also finds it compelling upon completion that they are in the epistemological state of absolute knowing; (2) That what Hegel is claiming is the mind of Spirit, is actually the mind of Spirit and not merely the reasoning of his own mind. Although, I find both of these aspects of Hegel's methodology questionable—and the questionable nature of both aspects motivate me to question whether the skepticism rendered in the *Phenomenology of Spirit* is more formidable than the solution to such skepticism—I only explore the latter questionable aspect in this book. From the latter questionable aspect, the third skeptical discovery presents itself, i.e., it is unclear that one is able to distinguish whether what Hegel is offering to his readers is in fact the mind of Spirit, or rather if it is merely a product of his own reasoning. It is because of this indistinguishability in the solution to arbitrariness that Hegel provides, I find it warranted to take the two aforementioned skeptical discoveries with greater seriousness than Hegel scholars (who are often aiming to explain what Hegel said or meant) often do, and claim that what Hegel said, that is helpful to philosophers after Hegel (or rather that the epistemological situation one is in after reading the *Phenomenology of Spirit*), is that there is an indistinguishability between the arbitrary and non-arbitrary nature of things.

After arguing this to be our epistemological situation, I proceed (in the final chapter) to examine contemporary phenomena with the intent to see if any phenomena add credence to this epistemological situation. My rationale for this examination is that, although I find the *Phenomenology of Spirit* has brought the possibility of this epistemological situation to light, it is not necessarily the case that this epistemological situation would be a compelling probability to consider, unless one could identify phenomena in our shared existence that appeared to indicate that this epistemological situation was more than merely a philosophical possibility, but rather was in fact the case. The two phenomena I examine and find to add credence to this epistemological situation are the placebo effect and the use of sensoriums in phenomenological anthropology. Concerning the placebo effect, I argue that arbitrary substances or treatments which contain no medicinal properties or value, when placed in particular contexts appear to contain a certain measure of medicinal value, when in fact they should not (given the current paradigm of medical materialism). Furthermore, although the FDA requires medical substances and treatments to outperform placebos in placebo test trial, no convincing explanation has ever been provided as to why placebos work in the first place given the view that the nature of substances and treatments are non-arbitrary.

Concerning the phenomena of the use of sensoriums in phenomenological anthropology, I argue that sensoriums are the sensory apparatus most compatible with the idea that perception begins in the subject and ends in the object, and not vice versa. Furthermore, given the fact that sensoriums are fashioned in particular ways such that there is no precultural, universal mode of perception, and that perception of objects is contingent upon particular sensoriums, I argue it would be difficult—if not impossible—to determine whether the empirical nature of an object, which one perceives is part of the non-arbitrary nature of that thing, or rather if it is part of the arguably arbitrary nature of one's sensorium. My rationale for examining these two phenomena is not to claim that after such examination one would be fully convinced that our epistemological situation is the aforementioned agnosticism; rather I aim to add a reasonable amount of cogency to the likelihood of this epistemological situation—as well as arguing that this particular epistemological situation has its origin in Hegel's *Phenomenology of Spirit*.

How Hegelian Agnosticism Is Developed

In the first chapter, I examine Hegel's topsy-turvy philosophical thought-experiment, as a critique of the Kantian position through an argument by ridicule. I review both the epistemological position which Hegel views Kant as holding and the epistemological uncertainty in which Hegel sees the Kantian phenomenal/Noumenal distinction as providing. I explain how Hegel sees this epistemological uncertainty leading to both metaphysical uncertainty concerning the possible disparity between what a thing appears to be in the phenomenal world, and what it may actually be in the Noumenal world. I then analyze Hegel's proposed solution to this uncertainty caused by the phenomena/Noumena distinction. After exploring Hegel's solution to the skepticism fostered by Kantian epistemology, I suggest that a greater skeptical concern remains—that concern being that what is arbitrary and what is universal need never contradict. Lastly, I explore how the critique of the topsy-turvy world is not only a critique of the phenomena/Noumena distinction but equally a critique of coherence epistemologies.

In the second chapter I explore how this compatibility between universality and arbitrariness relates to inductive reasoning via custom and habit in Hegel's analysis of Reason and Spirit I argue that Hegel shows his awareness of this inadequacy in inductive reasoning by essentially poking fun at the human tendency to make false inductive claims based on hasty generalizations, anecdotal evidence, and post hoc, ergo propter hoc fallacies. The topics I examine in detail in this chapter are Hegel's treatment of physiognomy and phrenology and the fallacious reasoning patterns that he compares these subjects (what we would now call pseudoscience) to. I then examine how Hegel appears to provide further speculation concerning how such claims would continue to be perpetuated in the consciousness of those who believed them true.

In the third chapter Hegel's methodology is further questioned. The epistemological concern becomes the following question: If we believe that it is epistemologically possible to share the mind of Spirit through comprehending the totality of Spirit's work through history, then how do we know that Hegel is sharing the mind of Spirit with us, and not merely his own point of view? This question, I argue, is the third skeptical discovery that the *Phenomenology of Spirit* inadvertently elucidates when Hegel attempts to demonstrate that all the forms of reasoning and ethical life that he has described are non-arbitrary and serve to indicate teleological aspects of Spirit. When analyzing the skepticism which this third discovery provokes, I also examine Eric Voegelin's thesis that in his writing of the *Phenomenology of Spirit*, Hegel is practicing sorcery. My purpose for including an examination of Voegelin's thesis in this chapter is not to defend Voegelin's polemical claims but merely to elucidate the fact that the third skeptical discovery is a necessary step one must take before making the type of claims Voegelin does.

In the fourth chapter I consider the combined implications of the three skeptical discoveries, and I demonstrate that the combined implications provide an epistemological situation in which the arbitrary nature of a thing is indistinguishable from the non-arbitrary nature of a thing.

INTRODUCTION

As a way of illustrating the foundation of this epistemological situation, I utilize the first skeptical worry which Descartes provides his reader in *Meditations on First Philosophy*, i.e., the example of the "insane" who both seems to empirical perceive things that are not there and believe things about themselves which are not true. Here I suggest that in the topsy-turvy world thought-experiment one can easily imagine that what is sane in the phenomenal world is insane in the noumenal world and vice-versa, and that what neither Descartes' example nor Kant's phenomenal/noumenal distinction considers is that the shared verifiability of empirical experience and the beliefs about such empirical experiences can be both arbitrary and universally shared within a particular milieu.

After presenting the way in which this first skeptical discovery allows for the possibility that the nature of things are arbitrary, I show how the following two skeptical discoveries make distinguishing whether something is non-arbitrary quite difficult and perhaps even impossible. The argument I will present is that the reasoning one adopts considering their empirical experiences as well as the beliefs they hold about such experiences, though it may appear internally coherent to the individual, may in fact be arbitrary. It is in this chapter that I also argue that Hegel demonstrates just how problematic the inadequacies of inductive reasoning can be, particularly when he presents such flawed systems of reasoning such as phrenology, physiognomy, and palmistry and compares such fallacious systems of reasoning to informal inductive fallacies such as hasty generalizations, anecdotal evidence, and post hoc, ergo propter hoc fallacies. I argue that to quite a large extent, Hegel shows us that systems of reasoning which contain contradictions can persist in societies where inductive fallacies are employed to the extent that the system of reasoning is never subject to falsifiability—or in milieus where certain beliefs are just too important to challenge, i.e., everywhere. Lastly, I argue that if the reasoning behind adopting this mind or the reasoning of this mind contains inductive fallacies, which contribute to its lack of falsifiability, then the system of reasoning may in fact be arbitrary. As an example of how inductive fallacies can contribute to a lack of falsifiability I look at the *Phenomenology of Spirit*, and the possibility that Hegel may assume the very thing he is aiming to prove (i.e., that Spirit is revealing itself in history for the benefit of humanity) and that given this assumption, the claim is almost impossible to falsify, particularly if one already believes it. It is here, after examining the compounded effects of these three skeptical discoveries that I conclude that it is quite difficult and perhaps not possibility to distinguish the arbitrary nature from the non-arbitrary nature of things.

In the final chapter I examine our current milieu with this agnosticism concerning the nature of things and ask whether there are any phenomena in our current milieu that adds credence to the idea that this agnosticism accurately captures our epistemological situation. The two phenomena which I argue add credence to this idea that this agnosticism accurately captures our epistemological situation are the placebo effect and the use of sensoriums in phenomenological anthropology. Concerning the placebo effect, I argue that when substances or procedures which should have absolutely no medical benefit are used as placebos (e.g., sugar pills or saline solution) and do produce medical benefit, the result could indicate a degree of arbitrariness in the nature of the thing (substance or procedure) used. Although placebo test trials necessitate that the medical procedure or drug must outperform the placebo, it still remains unclear why placebos work at all; as well as why, according to some research, as the efficacy of many pharmaceutics increases, the efficacy of the placebo effect also appears to be increasing.[18] In this chapter I argue that the phenomenon of the placebo effect adds credence to the agnosticism concerning the indistinguishability between the arbitrary and non-arbitrary nature of things.

The second phenomenon I examine is the use of sensoriums in phenomenological anthropology.[19] Here I argue that because sensoriums (according to phenomenological anthropologists) suggest both that perception begins in the subject and ends in the object (and not vice-versa) and because sensoriums are an embodied aspects of a culture or society's history and social practices, and can therefore differ from one milieu to

18. Beauregard, *Brain Wars*, 38–41.

19. The phenomenological anthropologist Kathryn Linn Geurts writes, "The definition of sensoriums is scientific in context, and aims to denote that the bodily apparatus for sensing should be viewed as an integrated whole system. In their book, *Brain, Symbol and Experience*, Laughlin, McManus, and D'Aquili provide such a definition of sensorium, explaining, 'The sensorium is the functional space within the nervous system wherein the phenomenal aspects of the cognized environment are constituted and portrayed in moment-by-moment experience. The sensorium, a time-honored term in science and medicine (Newton used the term in the eighteenth century!) usually refers to the "whole sensory apparatus of the body" (*Dorland's Illustrated Medical Dictionary*, 23rd ed.). *Phenomenal experience* is a construction mediated by the moment-by-moment reentrainment of perceptual and associative structures.... Phenomenal reality is thus in part an entrainment of cognitive and sensorial networks, which is designed to portray an unfolding world of experience to the organism. The functional space within which association and perception are combined into unitary phenomenal experience is the sensorium.'" Quote taken from Geurts, *Culture and the Senses*, 253.

another, that perception is contingent on the sensorium of the subject. From this acknowledgment of the contingent nature of perception, I question whether there is a single uniform empirical way of viewing an object. I argue that sensoriums suggest that there is not a single uniform precultural modality of the senses that allow for a uniform empirical experience of objects among people, but rather that the experience of an object or thing, is first an experience of (or is an experience mediated by) one's sensorium. Furthermore, ones sensorium, I argue, appears to be rendered by the embodiment of one's culture, values, and history—or a sensorium, to borrow a phrase of Bourdieu's is "history turned into nature." Given that empirical experience is either rendered or mediated by sensoriums, and that sensoriums themselves are rendered in a contingent fashion, I argue that the phenomenon of sensoriums adds credence to the agnosticism that an indistinguishability between the arbitrary and non-arbitrary nature of things accurately captures our epistemological situation.

1

The Universal, the Arbitrary, and the Topsy-Turvy

Remaining Agnostic Given Hegel's *Phenomenology of Spirit* and Coherence Epistemologies

Introduction: Varieties of Interpretation concerning Hegel's Topsy-Turvy World

WHEN APPROACHING HEGEL'S THIRD section of the *Phenomenology of Spirit*, "Force and Understanding," Hegel scholars appear to agree on one thing only: That these passages may be some of the most difficult of Hegel's writings to understand. Hegel has, in the previous two sections ("Sense Certainty" and "Perception") provided criticism of common epistemologies of his time; he has critiqued ways of knowing which rely on the certainty we place in the senses, as well as our perception, particularly concerning multimodal sensory objects. Both of these ways of knowing generally fall within the philosophical position of realism. In the third section, he provides a critique of the understanding, while also having his reader transition from consciousness to self-consciousness. This section is quite complex for a few distinct but related reasons. First, Hegel must show how understanding is the result of consciousness's inadequacies with perception. Second, Hegel must show the inadequacies with understanding—and this task involves three very different, dynamic concepts. The first concept is "Force"; the second concept is "Infinity"; and the third concept is "the topsy-turvy world." Thorough commentaries will, therefore, have to provide an explanation of what Hegel finds inadequate with the Understanding, while at the same time explaining how Hegel's nuanced ideas of Force, Infinity, and

THE UNIVERSAL, THE ARBITRARY, AND THE TOPSY-TURVY

the topsy-turvy world, help the reader to realize the inadequacies of the Understanding. After this task is accomplished, the commentator must then explain how this dynamic realization leads the reader to transition from consciousness to self-consciousness.

In this chapter we clarify what Hegel finds to be inadequate about the Understanding and how this inadequacy relates to Force as well as to Hegel's nuanced notion of Infinity. We then explore ways in which Hegel's reference to the topsy-turvy world has been understood by various commentators. What makes this task concerning the topsy-turvy world particularly interesting is that although the various commentators provide what they find as compelling explanation for what the topsy-turvy world might be directly referencing, no commentator finds the explanations of former commentators irrelevant or mutually exclusive. This is to say that the various commentaries view their comments as supplementary or additive to an overall manifold explanation of what the topsy-turvy world might be in reference to. Some such explanations include the topsy-turvy world to be understood in reference to Plato and the Allegory of the Cave, the doctrines of Christianity, Kant's phenomena/Noumena distinction, Descartes' evil genius, and Tieck's play *Die verkehrte Welt*. The topsy-turvy world has also been seen as an indirect critique of coherence epistemologies. After exploring these various interpretations of what the topsy-turvy world might be in direct reference to, we show how many of these explanations serves to provide a critique of coherence epistemologies and of multimodal objects.

The Inadequacies of Perception with an Emphasis on Multimodal Objects (or Things)

Hegel begins his section on perception with initial clarifications on the nature of a thing—and he often vacillates between the term "thing" and "object" when describing that which is being perceived by the subject. He describes the thing, to a limited extent, as the universal, and in doing so, he relates the thing back to the universal character of phenomena of "Here" and "Now," in which he earlier showed the inadequacies of sense certainty because sense certainty was unable to account for the universal aspect of what was being sensed. What Hegel aims to clarify early on, in his section on Perception, is that the essential nature of the object is neither the collection of properties which the object possesses, nor is it the multimodal experience which the object provides to the subject.

The nature of an object for Hegel is expressed in that it is a universal, particularly, a "mediated universal." The object's universal nature is mediated for us, the perceiver, in our perceptual experience of an object with variegated properties, but in our meditate experience we do not experience the complete nature of the universal as a concept whose properties can be instantiated by indefinitely many objects. It, again, is important to Hegel to note that the universality which contains the various determinate properties we experience as a multimodal object, is different from the properties themselves, as we experience them with our various modalities working in cooperation. Hegel expresses this distinction saying, "But the simple, self-identical universality is itself in turn distinct and free from these determinate properties it has. It is pure relating of self to self, or the *medium* in which all these determinacies are, and in which as a *simple* unity they therefore interpenetrate, but without *coming into contact* with one another; for it is precisely through participating in this universality that they exist indifferently on their own account."[1]

Before Hegel addresses the phenomenon of deception, which the perceiver is not immune to, he further clarifies three interrelated aspects of the object, which are perhaps best understood as in a process of relation to each other. This relation within the object is between what it is and what it is not. Not grasping the totality of these processes in the object, is not understood by Hegel as deception, but rather it is understood as an inadequacy of perception as a mode of knowing, in which he will later make clear to the reader that the Understanding has greater potentiality for apprehending the internal process/structure of the object more fully. To clarify, Hegel finds that the internal process/structure of the object of perception involves: (1) The universal medium in which the properties of an object are unified but do not come into conflict with each other; (2) The determinate negativity which does not conflict with the properties but excludes other contradictory properties and in the process provides a unity of the various determinate properties; (3) The multifarious properties that arise from the first two processes/structures interacting with each other (these ideas are provided by Hegel in para. 115). The criticism, therefore, that Hegel makes of perception is that it only allows the perceiver to view this aforementioned third moment of the object—as a thing and its properties—and not the former two essential processes/structures of the object, which is what the object is and which is what makes the multimodal perceptional experience possible.

1. Hegel, *Phenomenology of Spirit*, 67.

THE UNIVERSAL, THE ARBITRARY, AND THE TOPSY-TURVY

"Multimodal perception experience" is not a phrase which Hegel himself used—I wish he had, but—instead he offered descriptions such as: "All of these many properties [Hegel is referring to his example of salt] are in a single simple 'Here', in which, therefore, they interpenetrate; none has a different Here from the others, but each is everywhere, in the same Here in which the others are. And, at the same time, without being separated by different Here, they do not affect each other in this interpenetration."[2] The perceptional experience that is most used by Hegel, which is multimodal in nature is the object, salt. The subject (perceiver) in these examples of Hegel's experiences the properties of salt (as Hegel describes it) as "white and also tart, also cubical in shape, of a specific gravity," etc.[3]—and yet also unified in a single object which is salt. A few phenomenological features of a multimodal object as it is being perceived by a subject, I can only assume, Hegel found fascinating. He also found it necessary to elucidate these features, so that his readers might apprehend the inadequacies of perception as a way of knowing. The first point of fascination is that the object which is experienced by the subject through various sensory modalities, in reality possesses a unity. This is a unity which he will later describe as the object's Force. Hegel refers to this unity of an object as "a One" and describes the feature of the thing which holds the differentiation of the various properties of the thing together as the thing's "thinghood." In this section the "thinghood" corresponds to the first two aforementioned processes/structures which make the multimodal sensory experience possible, but in the following section, Hegel explains that this feature of a thing which holds these various properties together, in the same perceptual experience, without blending or excluding them is understood as "Force," i.e., an internal force which the thing possesses (and Hegel's example of the positive and negative distinctions within the unity of electricity is a helpful illustration for grasping antithetical distinction within overarching unity).

Hegel is also aware of the possibility of deception, and even entitles this section "Perception: Or the Thing and Deception" but he finds that the incorrect experience of the object is to be understood as an error in the subject and not in the object's thinghood or force. It is worth elaborating on this distinction further, given the attention which contemporary philosophies of the senses have paid to phenomena such as multimodal illusions and synesthesia. With regard to deception, Hegel writes, "If

2. Hegel, *Phenomenology of Spirit*, 68.
3. Hegel, *Phenomenology of Spirit*, 68.

consciousness itself did anything in taking what is given, it would by such adding or subtracting alter the truth. Since the object is the True and universal, the self-identical, while consciousness is alterable and unessential, it can happen that consciousness apprehends the object incorrectly and deceives itself."[4] Multimodal illusions such as the sound-induced flash illusion,[5] provide the subject with the false perception that a particular sound carries with it a particular image or shape. Synesthesia, on the other hand, blends two modalities of an object such that an object is experienced as possessing an additional property made available to the perceiver in a modality which would not usually be utilized.

An example should clarify any uncertainty the aforementioned statement may have caused. Let us use the example of an apple instead of salt, because we will utilize the color red for this example as well as the shape of the apple. Let us now suppose that when a synesthete perceives an apple (this particular apple being red and sweet and round—or apple-shaped) the synesthete also experiences a high-pitched sound, which is taken to be a property of the apple, just like the redness, and the sweetness, and the apple-shapedness are taken to be the properties of the apple. However, it is not the property of the apple intrinsically, but is experienced by the synesthete when the redness and the apple-shape are encountered in combination. This additional property of the apple, which the consciousness of the synesthete provides to the perceptional experience of the object, qualifies as deception given the Hegelian criteria. Let us describe this deception using Hegelian terminology: The structures/processes of the apple, i.e., its universal medium in dynamic relation with its determinate negation, makes possible an object with the qualities of redness, and sweetness, and apple-shapedness, but excludes from its unity the property of a high-pitched sound due to the particular force of the object. This particular high-pitched sound, nevertheless is perceived by the synesthete, in the particular "Here" of the multimodal object which is the apple—and in perceiving the high-pitched sound as part of the "Here" of the object, deception occurs in the subject.

Very troubling epistemological concerns becomes evident with the problem of deception, and with the particular example, I provided of the

---

4. Hegel, *Phenomenology of Spirit*, 70.

5. For a comprehensive account of the sound-induced flash illusion, refer to Abadi and Murphy, "Phenomenology of the sound-induced flash illusion"; Shams et al., "Visual Illusion Induced by Sound."

synesthete's deception. Hegel is aware of these concerns and finds that a turn to the epistemological approach of the Understanding in conjunction with the concept of Force, allows his reader to make necessary epistemological progress from consciousness to self-consciousness. Before we address the insights Hegel supplies in order to demonstrate to his reader the necessity of the progression, it may be helpful to elaborate on the range of this deception. Winfield explains that Hegel was not the first person to realize this internal contradiction in perception, or to use the idea of force in an attempt to resolve this contradiction. Winfield notes, "Locke recognizes that properties, as simple ideas, have no mediated content that could secure any connection to one another, let alone to any particular substrate that might possess them. We just happen to find them in conjunction with one another. Locke realized that if we want to make their togetherness something objective, rather than mere coincidence or subjective association, we need to introduce force."[6] Lastly, Winfield advises with respect to both Locke and Hegel's use of understanding, and to the utilization of the concept of Force for the problem of making perception something objective, that "We need to understand the thing to have the power to hold those sensuous properties under its sway, that is, to be the encompassing force whose expression is their united differentiation."[7] But the epistemological worry of deception still remains despite our appeal to the concept of Force, because of phenomena like synesthesia. Phenomena like synesthesia demonstrate that the perceiver has the ability to bring together additional properties into their perceptional experience of an object despite the fact that the unified differentiation of the object does not contain such properties. This does not preclude the empiricist position that the object possesses an objective set of properties, but the possibility which the particular phenomenon of synesthesia poses does complicate our epistemological reliance upon empirical knowledge as revealing only such properties of objects.

Put another way: What good is an appeal to objectivity, if deception potentially separates us from experiencing objects' objectivity (i.e., without our subjective consciousness adding or subtracting from the multimodal experience that the object provides)? Hegel does not use the example of synesthesia because it is likely he was not aware of its variegated manifestations, and because his topsy-turvy world makes the same point about deception much more forcefully. Before we move to an examination of Force and the

---

6. Winfield, Hegel's "Phenomenology of Spirit," 64.
7. Winfield, Hegel's "Phenomenology of Spirit," 65.

Understanding, I want to make two additional points concerning the grave epistemological concerns deception causes. Deception causes the following two questions to arise: (1) How do we know that one or more of the properties of an object which we experience in the multimodal perceptual experience of the object is actually a property of the unified differentiation of the object, and not an addition (a deception) supplied by our perceiving consciousness? (2) How do we know that the multimodal perceptual experience of the object we perceive are accurate perceptions of the object's properties, and not as Hegel imagines, the inverse of those very properties? If commenters are drawn to comment on any epistemological uncertainty, which Hegel's topsy-turvy world passage gives rise to, it is the uncertainty which arises from the latter question and not the former; however, given Hegel's understanding of perception as well as his acknowledgment of deception, the former epistemological worry remains unabated.

The Understanding, Force, and Law as Each Relate to the Nature of the Thing

Hegel's focus on the Understanding as opposed to perception begins as early as the second chapter of the *Phenomenology*, when he discusses the ostensible distinction between a thing and its properties, and the unity of a thing which is different from a thing and its properties. Concerning this apparent distinction, Hegel writes, "These pure determinatenesses [i.e., "the One of the properties" and "the Also of the 'free matter'"] seem to express the essential nature itself, but they are only a 'being-for-self that is burdened with a 'being-for-another.' Since, however, both are essentially in a single unity, what we now have is unconditioned absolute universality, and consciousness here for the first time truly enters the realm of the Understanding."[8] One is able to observe from Hegel's description of these determinatenesses, that what is necessary for a more thorough understanding of the thing, is the Understanding. The Understanding, according to Hegel allows one to apprehend, the single unity of the thing, which perception does not allow for, because perception only perceives the thing as an object with its manifold properties; whereas the understanding allows for universality of the object to be comprehended. Perception does not allow for an apprehension of the unity of an object, particularly because it is unable to perceive how the former determinateness, i.e., "the Also of the free

---

8. Hegel, *Phenomenology of Spirit*, 76–77.

matters" is unified with the latter determinateness, which is "the One of the properties." Perception cannot comprehend this process/structure, whereas, in Hegel's estimation, the Understanding can. For Hegel, the nature of the thing, in his paradigm of Absolute Idealism, becomes synonymous with the nature of the Understanding which grasps this process/structure, and is the nature of the thing. This means that the Understanding and the thing possess the same categorical structure, or as Findlay explains, "The nature of the Thing is therefore simply the nature of the Understanding, which constitutes it, and in which all these tensions are always present."[9]

After Hegel explains why it is necessary to move from the perception as a way of knowing, to the Understanding as a way of knowing, he explains that this movement of the object between the two aforementioned determinatenesses is properly understood as Force. In the beginning of the third section of the *Phenomenology*, Hegel explains Force as "the 'matter' posited as independent directly pass over into their unity, and their unity directly unfolds its diversity, and this once again reduces itself to unity. But this movement is what is called Force. One of its moments, the dispersal of the independent 'matters' in their [immediate] being, is the expression of Force; but Force, taken as that in which they have disappeared, is Force proper, Force which has been driven back into itself from its expression."[10] Force is understood as this dual determinateness of the object, and as the relatedness between the two determinatenesses. Force is the universal medium in which the particular properties of the object are unified but continue to possess and express their distinctness; Force is also the Oneness of the object which holds such variegated properties together in their unity. Force as process cannot be grasped by perception and, for Hegel, Force requires the Understanding to grasp the nature of the thing, which itself is Force. The Concept of Force is a concept belonging to the Understanding and not to perception.

Hegel provides his reader with many examples which appear to contain both this dual aspect of Force, not available to Perception, but rather available to the Understanding, and the unity of the object, which is also available to the Understanding and not to perception. One of Hegel's most often repeated examples, one which he will later build upon, is the example he provides of electricity. Concerning electricity, Hegel explains

9. Found in Analysis of Text for the *Phenomenology of Spirit*. Miller, *Phenomenology*, 512.
10. Hegel, *Phenomenology of Spirit*, 81.

that "*simple* electricity [by "simple electricity" Hegel means electricity that is not divided by the Understanding into its positive and negative aspects, and then further understood by the Understanding in those positive and negative aspects as obeying certain laws which make those aspects intelligible], e.g. is Force; but the expression of difference falls within the law; this difference is positive and negative electricity. . . . Electricity, as simple Force, is indifferent to its laws—to be positive and negative; and if we call the former its Notion but the latter its being, then its Notion is indifferent to its being."[11] Hegel uses this example of electricity as a way of departing from perception and bringing his reader to the mode of knowing which is, the Understanding. With this example of electricity, Hegel compares the Understanding and Perception as modes of knowing, and he elucidates the inadequacies of perception for not truly grasping what electricity is. Let us acknowledge the elucidations and comparison which Hegel makes here. As we depart from Perception we are provided with the dual determinateness of the thing (its diversity of properties and its unity); for Hegel, Force captures this dual determinateness in the structure of the Understanding. The diversity of the properties of a thing can be seen (or represented) in the non-simple Force of electricity, i.e., in electricity as differentiated by the Understanding into positive and negative electricity. These properties of electricity (positive and negative) belong to its being rather than its Concept or (Notion), and are grasped by the conceptual determinations which belong to the Understanding. The unity of a thing is seen (or represented) by what Hegel refers to as simple Force, or electricity understood as neither positive nor negative, but rather as a unity of both. Through the concept of Force (and the laws which apply to it) the Understanding apprehends electricity as both of these Forces in flux.

Hegel has yet to make clear whether we should continue to refer to a thing or object as "a thing," or rather if it would be more appropriate to refer to what we were formerly referring to as "things" (when we were in the epistemology of Perception), as "Forces" now that we have entered the epistemology of the Understanding. Hegel provides some insight when he transitions from electricity to a "single occurrence of lightning," but before we explain this transition, allow me to put forth a question, which I find makes the transition from thing to Force (and ultimately to Concept) somewhat confusing. If we suppose the example of the apple again in the epistemology of Perception, we can attribute sensible properties to

---

11. Hegel, *Phenomenology of Spirit*, 93.

it such as redness, and sweetness, and appleshapedness. But now using the Understanding, could we not also say that another property which the apple has is a center of gravity? And this center of gravity is a law, in which its essence is Force. But in acknowledging this we explain only that some properties of a thing are accessible via Perception (such as redness) while other properties of things are accessible via the Understanding (such as a center of gravity). We do not concede that the object is better grasped by the Understanding as dual determinate Forces in flux. Hegel advocates the latter approach to comprehension, which appears to create ambiguity between a law (or Force) which can aid one in understanding a property of an object, and explaining what was once an object as dual determinate Forces (or laws) in flux. This ostensible ambiguity remains in Hegel's example of "a single occurrence of lightning," which is developed from his earlier example of electricity.

In this example, Hegel explains that,

> The single occurrence of lightning, e.g., is apprehended as a universal, and this universal is enunciated as the law of electricity; the "explanation" then condenses the law into Force as the essence of the law. This Force, then, is so constituted that when it is expressed, opposite electricities appear, which disappear again into one another; that is, Force is constituted exactly the same as law; there is said to be no difference whatever between them. The differences are the pure, universal expression of law, and pure Force; but both have the same content, the same constitution. Thus the difference qua difference of content, of the thing, is also again withdrawn.[12]

In this example we see again an illustration, which Hegel uses for comparison; the difficulty of distinguishing whether a particular phenomenon it better understood as "a thing" or as "dual forces in flux" is now being compared to the similarity between Force and law, and Hegel claims that anything which can be said regarding Force can be likewise said regarding Law, so much so that any claims equating the two are tautological. (And here I gather that the same type of equating, which Hegel wishes his audience to find between Law and Force, he wishes his audience to find between Force and the Thing and its properties.) After this tautological admission is made, however, Hegel again shifts the reader's attention to the fact that although there is no distinction between Force and Law, the Understanding continues to make such a distinction, and not only makes this distinction but fluctuate between

---

12. Hegel, *Phenomenology of Spirit*, 94.

comprehending something such as a single occurrence of lightning, as Force, but also as Law. This fluctuation which the Understanding facilitates, Hegel refers to as "absolute flux," and it is by this absolute flux that the Understanding comprehends distinctions, which are only ostensible distinctions in that they are at the same time unity (such as the example, again of electricity, which can be understood as possessing both positive and negative aspects, or Forces, but also as a unity in which those aspects are in no way separate Forces but a single Force). It is with this awareness of absolute flux, that Hegel introduces his readers to the supersensible world, his nuanced notion of infinity, and his idea of a topsy-turvy world.

Infinity, the Supersensible World, and the Topsy-Turvy World

Hegel presents the supersensible world as a world that is shared by both the Notion of a thing and the Understanding. The fluctuation we inferred from appearance, between the "play of Forces" constituting an object, we posited to be intrinsic to the thing, but this, Hegel explains, was prior to our awareness of absolute flux. We understood Force (as intrinsic to the object) through the Understanding, but we understood Law as the product of the Understanding (i.e., as intrinsic to the Understanding). Absolute flux, which allows the Understanding to oscillate between using Force and using Law in its comprehension of an object, is seen by Hegel as a truth or law of the Supersensible World, as opposed to merely being an intrinsic truth of the object. This is because there is nothing so far that we have discovered in the object that allows for this flux, particularly given the unity of the object. The absolute flux, for Hegel, is experienced in the Understanding with regard to the object, and therefore belongs to the Supersensible World, in which both the Notion of a thing and the Understanding exist in relation to the objects we experience.

Hegel continues to analyze absolute flux, as it relates to appearance, but through the mode of knowing known as the Understanding (i.e., through laws), and he explains that in absolute flux there are two distinct laws in operation, and it is with these two laws that the Understanding can attempt to grasp the object. The first law, Hegel explains as the "law of appearance itself" and says that in this law "differences arise which are no differences, or that what is selfsame repels itself from itself; and similarly, that the differences are only such that as are in reality no differences and which cancel themselves; in other words what is not selfsame is self-attractive."[13] Conceptually speaking, this first law should be equally applicable and comprehendible to any of the various example phenomena Hegel has already provided, e.g., salt and electricity. However, representationally speaking, the law seems to lend itself more readily to the example of electricity than it does to salt. With respect to electricity, when Hegel explains that "differences arise which are no differences," this can be easily understood as the negative and positive aspects of electricity not really being different from each other in that both aspects are, in fact, a unity which is electricity. With the example of salt, which is white, bitter, and cubical in shape, these features do appear quite distinct, even though they do experience unity in the universality of the object. This may initially appear to reflect the real nature of the object in the supersensible realm, if not for the presences of absolute flux, which continues to complicate the question of what the object is? The differences, particularly in the case of salt, are made apparent in appearance, and are then understood in reference to the law of appearance.

Since it is flux, and not appearance, that he is analyzing, Hegel explains that it is the existence of a second law, which completes this flux the Understanding experiences when oscillating from Force to Law in its comprehension of phenomena. Hegel asserts that the second law is essentially the opposite of the first law, saying, "for this new law expresses rather that like become unlike and unlike become like. . . . The second is certainly also a law, an inner self-identical being, but a selfsameness rather of the unlike, a permanence of impermanence."[14] The first law (the law of appearances) is what took the unity of the object (or Force) and differentiated it into the various properties or aspects we experience in Perception. This second law, essentially collapses this differentiation back into unity—but, Hegel asserts that it does this in a very interesting way. This second law does this by attracting what is unlike (that is to say, what has been differentiated), back to its opposite. So, for example, if we image that salt experiences absolute flux and goes from unity to a phenomenal display of various properties, one such property being whiteness and another being bitterness, then in order for these determinate properties to be brought back into a unity (essentially completing a revolution in the infinite cycle of flux), the whiteness is brought back into the unity by its opposite, which is blackness, and likewise, the bitterness is brought back into unity by its opposite, which is

13. Hegel, *Phenomenology of Spirit*, 96.
14. Hegel, *Phenomenology of Spirit*, 96.

sweetness. What causes the unity of an object is the opposite or inverse of the properties which differentiate it.

In describing these two laws at work in the Supersensible World, Hegel acknowledges that the first law (which he references as "the tranquil kingdom of laws") corresponds to the world of appearances, the likes of which we encounter in Perception. With this first law corresponding to the world of appearances, Hegel relabels this law in reference to the supersensible, "the first supersensible world." This first supersensible world is what the Understanding utilizes when comprehending the world of appearance. The second law is also required to comprehend absolute flux, to which the world of appearance is only one movement in—and this second law, Hegel imagines also has its own world, which according to its law is the inverse of the first supersensible world. This second supersensible world is known as the inverted world (sometimes translated as the topsy-turvy world). If we attempt to imagine this inverted world sensibly it would be the opposite of the world of appearances, which we also perceive sensibly, and this would mean, as Hegel says, "if the one posited world is a perceived world, and its in-itself, as its inversion, is equally thought of as sensuous, then sourness which would be the in-itself of the sweet thing, is actually a thing just as much as the latter, viz. a sour thing; black, which would be the in-itself of white, is an actual black."[15] It seems that it is for didactic purposes that Hegel asks the reader to imagine the inverted world as having sensible properties, which are the opposite to the sensible properties of objects in the world of appearances. For as soon as we have imagined the inverted world as having sensible properties, Hegel reminds the reader that we are referring ultimately to absolute flux, and the Understanding's comprehension of an inner difference in an object, which is really a unity, but a unity that is in fluctuation as comprehended by the Understanding.

Comprehending the inverted world as a world of objects with sensible properties is somewhat misleading for Hegel, because he understands objects to be unities—unities of opposites which the Understanding experiences as flux between the two aforementioned laws. It is also somewhat misleading to view the world of appearance as ultimately having objects with sensible properties, or to treat such phenomena as exhaustive of what objects in the world are—to do this would be to ignore the totality of the object, which is the process of this flux. Lastly, it is not necessarily misleading, as much as it is disturbing to view the inverted world as having objects

---

15. Hegel, *Phenomenology of Spirit*, 98.

with sensible properties (even though, in the aforementioned quote, Hegel advocates for this as much as he does for viewing objects in the world of appearance in this manner) and this is because Hegel has consistently shown what we might call a metaphysical preference to the object as it exists in this form and in the parallel forms leading up to the ostensible division which are these two supersensible worlds. He shows this metaphysical preference to the unity or oneness of the object, as opposed to the diversity of its properties or "free matters."[16] He shows this metaphysical preference for Force proper, as opposed to the Force "unfolded into independent 'matters.'"[17] Now he is showing the same metaphysical preference for the object in the inverted world as opposed to the corresponding object in the world of appearance—referring to the former as "the in-itself." What is disturbing with regard to appearance and the metaphysical preference toward the inverted world as the "in-itself" is that it suggests the properties of an object are just as much the opposite of what they are in appearance. To make matters worse, Hegel does not restrict this idea to perceptual appearances, but includes in this idea ethical judgments as well.[18]

After describing these two supersensible worlds through law, and helping his reader to imagine them with opposite sensible properties, Hegel attempts to unify the object for the reader with his concept of infinity, which he describes as the unity of opposites.[19] Hegel further describes infinity, both as "absolute Notion" and as "absolute unrest of pure self-movement," and what these two descriptions of infinity share is that they both indicate the totality of the aforementioned processes of absolute flux, in which the Understanding's total experience of the object exists or takes place. What Hegel is sure to draw the reader's attention to is the distinction (or difference that is really no difference) that this process has shown to us, which occurs in the Understanding, concerning the object. This difference in sameness that is present within infinity, Hegel now argues is also present within self-consciousness—in that self-consciousness

---

16. Hegel, *Phenomenology of Spirit*, 76–77.

17. Hegel, *Phenomenology of Spirit*, 81–82.

18. With respect to how serious Hegel is being with his example of the topsy-turvy world, Gadamer explains that "it is in the chapter on 'Force and Understanding' where the thought-provoking and startling formulation, 'the inverted world' is to be found. Hegel is a Schwabian and startling people is his passion, just as it is the passion of all Schwabians." Gadamer, *Hegel's Dialectic*, 37.

19. Hegel describes it as "it is itself and its opposite in one unity." Hegel, *Phenomenology of Spirit*, 99.

distinguishes itself from consciousness, while at the same time not being different from consciousness. Describing this transition from consciousness to self-consciousness, as now the next necessary step in our attempt to grasp "a Thing," Hegel explains that "the necessary advance from the previous shapes of consciousness for which their truth was the Thing, an 'other' than themselves, expresses just this, that not only is consciousness of a thing possible only for self-consciousness, but that self-consciousness alone is the truth of those shapes."[20] Infinity is shared both by finite things and the finite self-consciousness; put another way, neither finite things nor the finite self-consciousness, is separate from the infinite, but possesses distinction as something finite, while existing within the infinite.

Acknowledging that the reality of the thing and the reality of self-consciousness share the same structure, categorically speaking, Hegel now takes the reader's attention from consciousness and places the reader's attention on self-consciousness. Hegel leaves the reader with one final distinction in this section, i.e., the distinction between "self-consciousness" and "consciousness in general." This is an important distinction we will examine shortly when we evaluate the relationship between universality and coherence epistemologies. Before we do this, however, it is advantageous to examine the many interpretations regarding Hegel's topsy-turvy world, and what these interpretations suggest both about the complexity of an object, and the complex structure and limitations of our epistemology as we attempt to grasp the truth concerning "a Thing."

Various Interpretations of the Topsy-Turvy World: Hyppolite, Gadamer, Flay, Solomon, and Verene

Jean Hyppolite is one of the first commentators on the *Phenomenology* to devote a section of text to an explanation of the topsy-turvy world. In 1946, in a work entitled, *Genesis and Structure of Hegel's* Phenomenology of Spirit, Hyppolite addresses the significance of the topsy-turvy world in a section entitled, "The Two Worlds and Their Dialectical Unity." In this section Hyppolite provides particular contents in the Gospels as a source of comparison and analogy to what Hegel is suggesting in the idea of the topsy-turvy world. Hyppolite understands that Hegel is ultimately emphasizing a unity in this section, but the opposites which are presented in the world of appearances and in the inverted world help the reader to

20. Hegel, *Phenomenology of Spirit*, 102.

answer the questions: What is being unified, or what opposition should be understood as a unity in these two worlds? Hyppolite paraphrases Hegel's presentation of such opposites, stating, "Thus, in the Gospels, what is honored in this world is scorned in the other; apparent strength is in fact weakness; hidden simplicity of the heart is in-itself superior to apparent virtue. In the Sermon on the Mount, Christ repeatedly opposes appearance—"it has been said"—to profound reality—"I say unto you." Hegel takes up this opposition of inner and outer and considers it in all its scope."[21] By providing the Gospels as a reference for a comparable inversion of phenomena given the existence of a supersensible reality, Hyppolite provides a basis for understanding what Hegel is possibly attempting to explain to his readers with the idea of the topsy-turvy world. In the Gospels, Hyppolite points to the conceptual reversals of certain ideas, such as strength and weakness, or honor and scorn. Phenomena which are portrayed in the Gospels in this way, are as Hyppolite rightfully points out, similar to what Hegel is saying of objects as understood in the topsy-turvy world, vis-à-vis the world of appearances.

Two matters of interest, which require further explanation (or clarification) from Hyppolite's comparison of reversals in the Gospels and Hegel's inverted world are: (1) Hyppolite correctly acknowledges that unlike the Gospels, "Hegel takes up this opposition of inner and outer and considers it in all its scope"; whereas the Gospels appear focused primarily on matters of ethics and matters pertaining to spirituality, Hegel applies this inversion to every imaginable opposite, e.g., black and white, bitter and sweet, north pole and south pole, etc. Because Hegel considers such opposition "in all its scope," I am inclined to remain somewhat skeptical concerning whether the comparison with the Gospels can help us to understand what Hegel is explaining to us by means of the topsy-turvy world, when the inversions do not relate to ethics or spirituality. (2) Hyppolite rightly explains with respect to the Gospels that when a comparison is made in which a reversal occurs—here I am particularly referring to what was explained concerning the Sermon on the Mount—a distinction between the two realities is made. Hyppolite refers to this distinction as "appearance (or it has been said)" and "profound reality (or I say unto you)." In the Gospels it is understood that there is an emphasis on what Hyppolite refers to as the "profound reality" so that one is able to distinguish between the appearance of virtue and virtue itself, or what appears to be weakness, but with regard to profound reality

---

21. Hyppolite, *Genesis and Structure of Hegel's "Phenomenology of Spirit,"* 136.

is, in fact, strength. It is again, somewhat unclear with respect to the scope of phenomena Hegel supplies in his examples how an epistemological priority to "profound reality" and away from "appearance" is supposed to be understood, both with respect to phenomena like black and white, or bitter and sweet, as well as to how one is to properly understand exactly how such opposites are supposed to be understood as a unity.

Hyppolite does not directly address either of these concerns, but rather suggests that the emphasis concerning what the topsy-turvy world is attempting to convey to the reader, should be understood to be on the ethical. With respect to this emphasis Hyppolite writes, "But Hegel passes from these examples borrowed from the science of his time [here Hyppolite is referring to the example which Hegel provides of opposition such as bitter and sweet, north and south poles of the magnet, and hydrogen and oxygen poles with respect to electricity] to spiritual examples, which in our opinion manifest the genuine meaning of this dialectic. He [Hegel] speaks in particular of the dialectic of crime and punishment ... punishment, which appears to dishonor a man, 'becomes in the inverted world the grace and the pardon which safeguard the man's essence and render him honor.'"[22] In explaining that spiritual examples are "the genuine meaning of this dialectic," Hyppolite essentially adds credence to his earlier comparison between the inverted world which Hegel is explaining, and the reversals pertaining to ethics and spirituality which the Gospels speak of. The fact that Hegel uses other examples of opposition from the sciences of his day and from the senses—examples which appear more difficult to relate to the Gospels in any straightforward way, does not seem to weaken the comparison between the Gospel reversals and the inverted world, for Hyppolite, because Hyppolite finds that the true meaning of the dialectic pertains to spiritual/ethical examples.

To solidify this emphasis of the dialectic on spiritual examples as opposed to examples from the senses or from the sciences, Hyppolite focuses on Hegel's explanation of crime and punishment, particularly on how such apparent opposition does in fact result in a unity. Describing how Hegel apprehends punishment as it relates both to appearance and to the inverted world, Hyppolite explains, "Punishment appears to be a vengeance externally imposed on the criminal; in fact, punishment is self-punishment. That which, viewed superficially, appears as a constraint is in its profound meaning a liberation. ... The difference between

---

22. Hyppolite, *Genesis and Structure of Hegel's "Phenomenology of Spirit,"* 136–37.

phenomenon and essence, between apparent meaning and hidden meaning, has become so profound that it destroys itself."[23] In this example of crime and punishment we are now able to see exactly how Hyppolite claims that the reversals which pertain to spiritual things that we find in the Gospel, relate to the spiritual/ethical examples which Hegel utilizes in explaining features of the topsy-turvy world. We also observe how the profound meaning of something like punishment relates to what punishment appears to be (here Hyppolite explains appearance as "viewed superficially" and sees the profound explanation as both reinterpreting the superficial view, and removing any prior distinction between the superficial appearance and the profound reality). We, however, are not provided any clear understanding of how the topsy-turvy world can be understood as it pertains to phenomena of the senses or to scientific distinctions within phenomena, but we are implicitly told that things (phenomena) are not the emphasis or "genuine meaning" of the dialectic.

Hans-Georg Gadamer has been credited with writing one of the most novel and thorough interpretations of Hegel's topsy-turvy world. This interpretation of Hegel's topsy-turvy world is entitled, "Hegel's 'Inverted World,'" and is found in chapter 2 of the work, *Hegel's Dialectic: Five Hermeneutical Studies*. In his interpretation of Hegel's topsy-turvy world, Gadamer, finds that Hegel is interested in addressing concerns in metaphysics and epistemology which are quite similar to the philosophical problems which are addressed in Plato's allegory of the cave, as well as with Aristotle's criticism of Plato's notion of *eidos*. In Hegel's explanation of the topsy-turvy world, Gadamer finds that Hegel attempts to provide a novel answer to this disagreement concerning the ultimate nature of objects; a disagreement which is first understood in Aristotle's criticism of Plato's idea of *eidos* being the true nature of objects. Gadamer also sees Hegel as understanding that the contributions of modern scientists, such as Galileo and Newton, articulate a worldview similar to that of Plato in respect to the fact that each explains that the world of appearances corresponds to a world of laws or ideas, and that these laws or ideas are unchanging, and that the world of appearances is an imperfect representation of these laws or ideas. When describing the world of appearances and the world of ideas or laws, in which the world of appearances imperfectly corresponds to, Gadamer find the views similar enough to refer to them collectively as the "Platonic-Galilean conception

---

23. Hyppolite, *Genesis and Structure of Hegel's "Phenomenology of Spirit,"* 137.

of the tranquil realm of laws or unitary lawfulness."[24] Gadamer interprets Hegel as acknowledging that these three thinkers relate the world of appearance to a world of laws, but Gadamer also understands Hegel to find (much like Aristotle takes issue with Plato) that much of what is empirically real is neglected in this understanding of ultimately reality or essence when it is understood as the "Platonic-Galilean conception of the tranquil realm of laws or unitary lawfulness." What is not accounted for in this understanding of reality, is the reality of change, and Gadamer understands the topsy-turvy world as Hegel's way of addressing the reality of change in the world. Gadamer also understands, that in criticizing this understanding of reality, which can, in part be attributed to the ideas of Plato, Hegel has shown a parallel dissatisfaction with the limitations of Plato's ideas, as Aristotle had previously shown in his criticism.

Describing how Hegel's inverted world relates both to the ideas of Plato and to Aristotle's criticism of Plato, Gadamer explains, "A world which contains the *arche kineseos*, and as such is the true world, is an inversion of Plato's world in which motion and alteration were supposed to be naught. This world too is supersensible. . . . This world is not just the tranquil realm of laws which all alternation must obey, rather it is a world in which everything moves because everything contains the origin of change in itself. That appears to be a pure reversal, and modern philosophical research has also struck upon the image of 'reversal' for Aristotle's reinterpretation of Plato doctrine of ideas."[25] For Gadamer, Hegel has understood Aristotle's criticism of Plato, as essentially a critique of Plato's rationale for doubling the world—for propounding that there is a supersensible world, which is unchanging, and which is somehow more real than the world of appearances. What Hegel finds to be most real, and what he finds has been neglected by Plato as well, is the principle of change itself. This principle of change, for Hegel is also supersensible and, according to Gadamer, Hegel uses the idea of the inverted world to contain, or rather, express this principle of change.

After describing the relevance of the inverted world, to the tranquil realm of laws—which Gadamer credits both to Plato and Galileo—and to the world of appearance (ultimately explaining that the inverted world contains what is most real, because it contains the principle of change), Gadamer investigates what more might be understood by the German word "*Verkehrte*" asking, "Why is the true reality called the *verkehrte*

24. Gadamer, *Hegel's Dialectic*, 44.
25. Gadamer, *Hegel's Dialectic*, 44–45.

world?"[26] Some of Gadamer's tentative conclusions involve exploring what he identifies as the double meaning of the word "*verkehrte*" as meaning both "inverted" and "perverted." Gadamer finds that Hegel utilizes both of these meanings in the idea of the topsy-turvy world, explaining that "The *verkehrte* world is thus a world in which everything is the reverse of the right world."[27] In acknowledging that this double meaning is being utilized by Hegel when he discusses the *verkehrte* world, Gadamer suggests Hegel's rhetorical style of argument could be classified as satire, if we acknowledge that "one of the main tasks of satire is to expose moral hypocrisy, i.e., the untruth of the world as it is supposed to be, the real trenchancy of *verkehrte* comes into view."[28] But Gadamer, in comparing the *verkehrte* world to satire, does not only wish to explore the possibility that Hegel is being satirical and shocking as he propounds that an inverted world contains what is most real; Gadamer also wishes to compare the *verkehrte* world to the idea of satire itself—which is a fascinating comparison—because as Gadamer rightly elucidates, "in every instance satirical portrayal is the 'opposite in itself.'"[29] Gadamer's commentary of the inverted world has provided the reader with helpful comparisons to understand both Hegel's possible style of argument, as well as phenomena in which to compare the idea of the inverted world to (e.g., satire itself). He also provides a larger philosophical context in which the inverted world can be seen as both a criticism of Platonic-Galilean understanding of ultimate reality, and to a certain extent, as an agreement with the criticism of Aristotle over the inadequacies of Plato's understanding of reality.

The next unique interpretation of the meaning of Hegel's topsy-turvy world is introduced by Joseph C. Flay in his article entitled "Hegel's 'Inverted World,'" and this interpretation is developed further by Robert Solomon, in a variety of articles and books, including, *From Hegel to Existentialism*, *In the Spirit of Hegel*, "Hegel's *Phenomenology of Spirit*," and "Truth and Self-Satisfaction." In his article, Flay is quick to acknowledge the former interpretations by Hyppolite and Gadamer, and explains, in a footnote, that his explanation should in no way be seen as contradictory, but rather as supplementary and not mutually exclusive. What Flay wishes to make clear is that although one can seek to understand the topsy-turvy

26. Gadamer, *Hegel's Dialectic*, 46.
27. Gadamer, *Hegel's Dialectic*, 48.
28. Gadamer, *Hegel's Dialectic*, 49.
29. Gadamer, *Hegel's Dialectic*, 49.

world through the comparisons that both Hyppolite and Gadamer provide, one might overlook important epistemological concerns if one does not take into account what the topsy-turvy world explains, given the work of Leibniz and of Kant.[30] Flay observes Hegel to understand that the ideas of Leibniz and the ideas of Kant relate to the concept of appearances and the first supersensible world differently. The terminology for such as distinction, which Flay understands Leibniz to use is *mundus intelligibilis* (first supersensible world) and *mundus sensibilis* (world of appearance). Flay explains Leibniz's epistemological understanding of how these two worlds relate quoting from Kant's *Critique of Pure Reason* (A270, B326) explaining, "'Leibniz erected an *intellectual system of the world*, or rather believed that he could obtain knowledge of the inner of things by comparing all objects merely with the understanding and with the sundered, formal concepts of its thought,' leaving 'sensibility . . . only a confused mode of representation . . . of the *thing in itself*.'"[31] Quoting from Kant's *Critique of Pure Reason* once more, Flay explains that Kant's view of the relation between sense-perception and the intelligible world is quite different, explaining "Kant has articulated an 'intelligible world' in which 'the condition of the objective employment of all our concepts of understanding is merely the mode of our sensible intuition, by which objects are given to us' (A286, B342) as a manifold."[32]

After providing the difference in understanding between the way in which Leibniz and Kant saw the world of appearances being distinguished from the intelligible world, Flay stresses that Hegel disagrees with how both thinkers understand this distinction, and he uses the topsy-turvy passage to explain both his own position, and what he finds to be disagreeable about the former two positions. What is disagreeable to Hegel is that neither grasps that the concept "as concept of the understanding is indeed the same as the inner of things"[33] i.e., neither position makes the move from consciousness to self-consciousness.[34] Since neither makes this move from

---

30. Here Flay explains, "Both [Hyppolite and Gadamer] have made sense of this passage, the former in a reference to Christian doctrine and the latter in a reference to Plato and Aristotle. My own attempt here to comprehend this passage in reference to Kant and Leibniz does not 'disagree' with either interpretation, but rather supplements these interpretations." Flay, "Hegel's 'Inverted World,'" 662.

31. Flay, "Hegel's 'Inverted World,'" 672.

32. Flay, "Hegel's 'Inverted World,'" 673.

33. Flay, "Hegel's 'Inverted World,'" 673.

34. This is not to say that self-consciousness does not play a vital role in the approaches

consciousness to self-consciousness (so that distinctions remain between the understanding and the inner nature of a thing), absurd results follow—results which the topsy-turvy world articulate—and this is particularly the case with the epistemological uncertainty that is the result of Kant's phenomena/noumena distinction. This is not to say that there is not distinction in Hegel's system, but rather that the distinction is not between appearance and the supersensible. Instead this distinction is an internal distinction and not one to be made between appearance and the supersensible; Flay explains as much by stating, "When, however, the distinction is made as it really now is—namely as internal distinction—the supersensible as supersensible disappears. It is *not* the case that sweet is sour, North Pole is South Pole, etc., but rather that they determine each other, necessarily standing in a self-defining relationship."[35] If, however, this distinction is not understood as internal, but rather as a distinction between the supersensible and that of appearance (such as the Kantian phenomena/noumena distinction) then it is the case that epistemological uncertainty is produced such that what appears to be the case in one world is, in reality, its opposite.

It is this aforementioned last point concerning the epistemological uncertainty of the phenomena/noumena distinction, which Robert Solomon continues to develop when interpreting the significance of the topsy-turvy world. Solomon finds that the Kantian phenomena/noumena distinction is both essential for understanding the relevance of Hegel's topsy-turvy world, and at the same time, that Hegel's topsy-turvy world serves to ridicule the Kantian distinction. In his article entitled "Hegel's *Phenomenology of Spirit*," Solomon explains that "the inverted-world passage is essentially an argument by ridicule, for what becomes evident is that, if we take Kant's notion of noumenon seriously, any sort of nonsense becomes equally intelligible. Either the noumenal world is just like the phenomenal world, or, not only does it not make sense to talk about it, but it does not even make sense to suppose that there might be one."[36] It is with Solomon's interpretation of the topsy-turvy world that we first find a very skeptical worry brought out against the Understanding as a way of knowing, particularly when there is a separation between the phenomenal experience of a thing

---

of Kant and Leibniz, but rather that Hegel finds both approaches, which involve the self-consciousness, will not bring the epistemological certainty that Hegel proposes absolute knowing will.

35. Flay, "Hegel's 'Inverted World,'" 676.
36. Solomon, "Hegel's *Phenomenology of Spirit*," 200.

and the thing as it is in itself (the noumenal). Solomon interprets Hegel as presenting this very profound skeptical worry concerning Kant's epistemology, in the form of ridicule, through the topsy-turvy world thought experiment. Solomon finds the topsy-turvy world to, therefore, provide an argument for the rejection of such an epistemological separation between the phenomenal and the noumenal, or between the finite and the infinite (i.e., what Hegel understands to be the bad infinite)—and he finds that this argument takes the form of ridicule, by showing the epistemological absurdities or uncertainties that would result from this separation of phenomena and noumena, which is the epistemological position of the Kantian system (according to Solomon's interpretation of Hegel). Passages in the topsy-turvy world section of Hegel's *Phenomenology of Spirit* which state contrast between the two worlds such as "this means that what in the law of the first world is sweet, in this inverted in-itself is sour, what in the former is black is, in the other, white,"[37] appear to provide evidence for such ridicule in Solomon's interpretation. Hegel finds, according to Solomon, that Kant's epistemology is so unsatisfactory, and he demonstrates this unsatisfactory nature by imagining that our phenomenological experience could be so mistaken that we are actually perceiving the exact opposite of what things actually are in themselves, in every respect. This is what Solomon interprets the main emphasis of the topsy-turvy world to be: It is a philosophical thought-experiment in which we are able to see the complete lack of certainty of the Kantian epistemology. Solomon's view of Hegel's characterization of Kant's epistemology, may resemble a straw man argument, if, in fact, it is an accurate understanding of what Hegel is attempting to do with the topsy-turvy world. We will, however, momentarily consider the merits of such ridicule, within the context of the idea of universality, as well as in conjunction with the contributions of Verene.

In his work *Hegel's Recollection: A Study of Images in the Phenomenology of Spirit*, Donald Phillip Verene, provides a few additional and interesting ways in which one is able to understand both the relevance of Hegel's topsy-turvy world, as well as what, in addition, the topsy-turvy world may be in particular reference to. His work does this directly in chapter four, which Verene entitles "The Topsy-turvy World" and indirectly in chapter seven of his work which is entitled "Phrenology." In the chapter "The Topsy-turvy World," Verene provides two additional insights into how to view the topsy-turvy world, given other literature and philosophical writing that Verene

37. Hegel, *Phenomenology of Spirit*, 97.

finds Hegel to be influenced by. Much like Flay, Verene acknowledges the varieties of interpretations of this particular passage which have already been supplied (including those of Hyppolite, Gadamer, Flay, Bossart, Zimmerman, and Solomon) both concerning what the topsy-turvy world is in reference to as well as its overall relevance to Hegel's system of *Wissenschaft*. Verene finds the similarity between what Hegel does in his section on the topsy-turvy world, particularly concerning the doubt that he engages with, and the awareness of self-consciousness as the means to alleviate much of this doubt, to be similar to—and to quite possibly be in reference to Descartes' *Meditations*. Exploring this idea, Verene explains:

> The understanding, drunk with its power, produces the concept of the reverse world. It forms the thought that there could be a world the reverse of the one it has secured by its distinction between appearance and reality or super-sensible world. In this thought it grasps that everything it has designated as appearance might just as well be the real and everything that it has designated the real might just as well be appearance. What I see before me may in reality be exactly opposite to what I see. The fact that I can articulate in consciousness the difference between appearance and non-appearance, that I can grasp these as two realms, destroys all possibility of certainty of sense and throws certainty back onto the I that makes the distinction. Through the absurdity of this twoness that goes nowhere, the self as something in itself is born. What we have here has a striking similarity to the end of the first Meditation in Descartes' *Meditationes de prima philosophia*. Hegel does not himself make this comparison, but it is too obvious not to consider as throwing light on the nature of the *verkehrte Welt*.[38]

Verene sees parallels between Hegel's topsy-turvy world and the doubt explained in Descartes' first Meditation, in the awareness that appearance may in no way correspond to reality, and that the way out of such uncertainty involves a turn to the self-consciousness. Concerning the first parallel, i.e., that appearance may in no way correspond to reality, we arrive at a somewhat different epistemological result than the way in which Hyppolite and Gadamer have been describing the way the topsy-turvy world corresponds to the world of appearances. It is the case that Hyppolite and Gadamer stress the opposite nature of the correspondence between the two world—for example what is white in one is black in another or what is bitter in one is sweet in another—Verene, and to a similar extent Solomon appear to stress

---

38. Verene, *Hegel's Recollection*, 41.

not the opposite nature between the two worlds, but rather they stress the epistemological uncertainty of the world of appearance and this uncertainty can be illustrated in the extreme through imagining that what something appears to be, is actually the opposite of what it is.

This focus on the uncertainty of things rather than on the opposite nature of things is also brought out in the second suggestion Verene makes concerning what Hegel's use of the topsy-turvy world may be in reference to. Verene explains that there is a possibility (though Verene is uncertain if any commentator before him has ever mentioned the connection) that "Hegel's *verkehrte welt* is connected with the play with the same name by Ludwig Tieck."[39] Verene is uncertain whether Hegel was aware of this particularly play but stresses the possibility, particularly because the play was published eight years before Hegel published the *Phenomenology of Spirit* (1799) and because many of the play's admirers were individuals that Hegel would have been familiar with, e.g., Schleiermacher, William Grimm, Eichendorff, and the Schlegel brothers.[40] Tieck's play (which was translated into English as *Land of Upside Down* by Oscar Mandel in 1978) has elements of absurdity, general lack of certainty concerning what reality is, and reversals (i.e., that things and people are the opposite of what they are taken to be).[41] This play also possesses what might be considered a fourth element related to, but nonetheless distinct from, the aforementioned three—the idea that what people think is real might actually be real simply because they think it is (at times appearing to collapse the distinction between fact and fiction). These elements within the play, coupled with the compelling possibility that Hegel may have been aware of the play, makes Tieck's play *Verkehrte Welt* a viable possibility for what Hegel's utilization of "the topsy-turvy world" might be in direct reference to.

Verene's remaining contribution to understanding Hegel's topsy-turvy world appears in chapter seven of the aforementioned text, entitled "Phrenology." In this chapter Verene aims to show what in particular, Hegel desires his readers to apprehend as he explores the topic of phrenology and to a

---

39. Verene, *Hegel's Recollection*, 50.

40. Verene, *Hegel's Recollection*, 50–51.

41. In the introduction to the translation of the play, Oscar Mandel describes some of the elements/dynamics of the play in the following way: "In the play the fictive audience is watching, the personages at one point sit down to watch a play, in which the personages once again gather to watch a play. The fictive audience is now in a whirl; the walls of reality seem to buckle; reality threatens to dissolve in dream; and one of the fictive spectators suddenly cries out, 'What if we were fiction too?'" Mandel, Introduction, 20.

lesser extent physiognomy in the *Phenomenology of Spirit*, as well as why it is that he attacks these forms of thinking so strongly. Verene proposes that Hegel saw phrenology as the opposite of phenomenology, explaining that "Phrenology is the inverted world, the upside-down version of phenomenology.... Phrenology must be attacked so strongly, as an illusion of consciousness in its road to self-knowledge, not simply because it is a pseudo-science and represents bad thinking, but because it is the natural opposite, the inversion of the true science of mind—phenomenology."[42] Verene's insight is quite fascinating, not only with respect to the question of why Hegel focuses so strongly on attacking phrenology, but also for how the idea of the topsy-turvy world can be seen as mediating or providing context for systems of understanding present in societies. In such an example we have two systems of thought existing side by side in a society, with the claim that one is the inverse of the other. This, I suggest, paints a unique picture of reality (one in which all former explanation of the topsy-turvy world have not explicitly considered); one in which there are not two worlds in which we are uncertain if the lesser world of appearance corresponds accurately to or may, on the other hand, appear as the opposite of the world as it is in itself. This picture suggests that both "worlds" or both "versions" exists in opposition in the same world (a world in which the opposition, itself, is the only distinction—as opposed to a distinction like phenomena/noumena).

A Topsy-Turvy World Critique of Coherence Epistemologies and of Multi-Modal Objects

In this section I aim to show how many of these aforementioned explanations of Hegel's use of the topsy-turvy world serve to provide a critique of coherence epistemologies and of the multimodal objects (or things) we experience because within these explanations, what is arbitrary has the possibility of being compatible with what appears to be universal in the phenomenological experience described. Let us begin by examining Solomon's suggestion that Hegel's use of the topsy-turvy world is a philosophical thought experiment that functions as an argument by ridicule against the Kantian philosophy (particularly against the phenomena/Noumena distinction). If we consider this argument by ridicule in relation to multimodal sensory objects we find that an object as it appears in the phenomenal world is opposite (and more generally speaking, different from) to what it

42. Verene, *Hegel's Recollection*, 89.

actually is in the Noumena world. We can now also imagine that such considerations as universality of perceptual experience (or any form of consensus among members of a society) ultimately adds no credence, nor offers any guarantees that what everyone experiences in the phenomenal world bares any resemblance to the Noumenal world. Furthermore, because Solomon's argument appears to emphasize the ridicule aspect of the topsy-turvy world as opposed to the inversion aspect, I find that one can conclude that skepticism is the result of the phenomena/noumena distinction according to this argument. We now for the first time observe what is meant by the idea that what is universal is compatible with what is arbitrary. Here it must be noted that this is not the point Hegel is ultimately attempting to make, but rather he is (according to Solomon) ridiculing Kant to make room for his own epistemological system of Absolute Knowing, which he aims to demonstrate can solve the epistemological uncertainty he has discovered in the Kantian system. According to this argument by ridicule the experience of a particular multimodal object is universally experienced as having particular properties, while in actuality this universal experience is in fact arbitrary in that it is not based on the actual thing as it is in itself. We might ask what causes this universal phenomenal experience which in no way corresponds with its object (Put another way: Is this universal experience contingent on anything?)—the answer to such a question Solomon appears to suggest is the very distinction itself, which is what, he suggests, is being ridiculed by Hegel. What remains from this interpretation is the skeptical worry that the universality of a multimodal experience is no guarantee of the epistemological accuracy of that experience.

Let us now, for a moment move away from multimodal objects, and observe forms of reasoning as they relate to the topsy-turvy world—here we will also consider the context of coherence epistemologies as they relate to systems of reasoning. Verene's suggestion that phrenology is the topsy-turvy version of phenomenology is quite relevant in that it allows us to move away from multimodal objects to forms of reasoning and then move to a critique of coherence epistemologies. Unlike the former example in which there is a uniform and universal lack of congruency between what a multimodal object appears to be and what it actually is, we have two different forms of reasoning existing side by side. Furthermore, neither form of reasoning is universally accepted by all the members of a particular milieu, rather some individuals believe in phrenology as an accurate form of reasoning why others after reading Hegel's work believe contrariwise that phenomenology is the accurate form of reasoning. This is to say that these two groups of individuals have differing webs of belief[43] with respect to their acceptance or rejection of the reasoning systems of phenomenology and phrenology. The question can now be asked concerning how both systems of reasoning can exist side by side, each making extremely different law-like claims about the connections of various events in the empirical world—one system of reasoning appearing cogent to some while the other form of reasoning appearing cogent to others. The answer to this question of how these two systems can exist side by side, each appearing more cogent than the other to their audiences, is that they are each part of different coherent epistemologies—and therefore, each system of reason is compelling to its audience because of its greater explanatory power for making sense of the world, which these individuals find themselves in.

The topsy-turvy world becomes a critique of coherence epistemologies because it is through a coherence epistemology that an individual is able to believe the exact opposite of what is the case—e.g., it is through a coherence epistemology that an individual believes that phrenology is an accurate way of reasoning; whereas (according to Verene's interpretation of Hegel) phrenology is actually the inverse of phenomenology, which is the accurate form of reasoning. To grasp what is being said by Verene's understanding of Hegel's attack on phrenology, a correspondence view of knowledge must be assumed—a correspondence view in which phenomenology provides one with an accurate system of reasoning that provides knowledge which would correspond to reality, i.e., to what is. At the same time coherence epistemologies must also be posited as being available to the mind and organizing forms of reason—but at the same time providing a form of reason which is the inverse of the form of reason which would provide the knowledge which would correspond to reality. Instead this knowledge system is the inverse of the correct system—this inverse according to Verene is the "knowledge system" of phrenology, and it is the inverse of phenomenology. It is through coherence epistemologies that the topsy-turvy world is made manifest in the empirical world and this is how the topsy-turvy world functions as an implicit critique of coherence epistemologies—coherence epistemologies have the ability to make the absurd world a reality to those operating within that coherent epistemology if that coherence epistemology either does not correspond to facts about the world, or if the coherence

---

43. Here I am using the term "web of belief" as it is presented and understood by Quine and Ullian in *Web of Belief*.

epistemology corresponds in an opposite way to such facts. This implicit critique of coherence epistemologies is acknowledged by Solomon in his work "Truth and Self-Satisfaction," where he explains that

> A frequent objection to the coherence theory is the following: any system of coherent beliefs can be turned into an equally coherent system by the systematic application of some logical operator, e.g., by turning each belief into its contradictory. That is, there might be equally coherent but mutually incompatible systems of belief, and it would not seem to make sense to say that they are both equally "true." This argument has its clear instantiation in the *Phenomenology*. Hegel offers us the absurd counter-example of a *"Verkehrte"* or "inverted" world, in which black is white, light is heavy, good is evil, and so on. His ultimate target is Kant's distinction between noumenon and phenomenon, but the example holds as well against coherence theory. It is a material equivalence of the replacement of each true proposition with its contradictory, and the result is absurd. Truth cannot be mere coherence. But neither, Hegel argues, can truth be divorced from our beliefs, from the categories or our "forms of consciousness."[44]

When we examine the combined insights of Solomon and Verene concerning how we are to understand the epistemological critiques that the topsy-turvy world provides, we are left with a skeptical worry concerning the coherence epistemology in which we are operating in—with respect to both the multimodal objects we perceive as well as the systems of reasoning we utilize to make the world make sense to us. It is unclear to what extent a coherence epistemology has either direct or indirect influence on our perceptions of multimodal objects (This will be a question take up in the final chapter). What remains clear, however, is that the universal experience of a particular object is no guarantee of that object's non-arbitrary nature. What is clear—and what we may refer to as our second skeptical worry—is that some coherence epistemologies may (at least in theory) correspond to facts about the world—whereas, Hegel and his commentators (I find correctly) suggest that other coherence epistemologies can correspond to the opposite of what is factual about the world—or perhaps may not correspond at all. The skeptical worry becomes how one knows which type their particular coherence epistemology is—whether the coherence epistemology which they subscribe to corresponds to facts about the world or rather is absurdity when referenced to facts about the world.

44. Solomon, "Truth and Self-Satisfaction," 704.

Hegel has unwittingly demonstrated in the *Phenomenology* that both possibilities are practicable and that the universality of experience within a particular coherence epistemology is no guarantee of a correspondence to the non-arbitrary nature of things. In the following chapter we will examine what Hegel's particular solutions are for coming to epistemological certainty, and whether such provided solutions are viable.

2

Reason, Phrenology, and Coherence Epistemologies

IN THIS CHAPTER WE will begin by reviewing the dialectical movements which have taken place in Hegel's *Phenomenology of Spirit* beginning with his turn toward self-consciousness and moving to his analysis and attack on phrenology. This review seeks to answer questions concerning what Reason's overall context is within the *Phenomenology* as well as to what extent phrenology can be understood to be representative of reason for Hegel in the movement of Spirit. After answering these questions we will explore Hegel's presentation and criticism of phrenology (as well as physiognomy and palmistry to some extent) which he shows to be based on faulty inductive reasoning such as hasty generalization, anecdotal evidence, lack of falsifiability and post hoc fallacies—and how this faulty inductive reasoning appears to be related to custom and habit in the sense which Hume described.[1] Following this examination of phrenology we will consider other questionable characteristics of this form of reasoning which earn it the classification of pseudoscience in our contemporary times, e.g., lack of falsifiability, lack of connectedness to other sciences and appeal to mystery. Given these questionable characteristics as well as its prevalence and general acceptance among many during Hegel's time, we explore the idea as to whether pseudoscience and Reason are different in kind or different in degree. With respect to our latter concern we explore this degree versus kind distinction within the context of coherence epistemologies and articulate

---

1. Here I have in mind what Hume expresses in the conclusion of his seventh chapter in his work *Enquires concerning Human Understanding* entitled "Of the Idea of Necessary Connexion."

our second skeptical worry—that given the existence of coherence epistemologies it appears uncertain how to determine to what degree one's system of reasoning bears any correspondence to actuality. This consideration also explores the possibility that it appears doubtful that such a determination can be independently described or specified.

From Self-Consciousness to the Prevalence of Phrenology during Hegel's Time

After Hegel takes the reader through the three forms/movements of consciousness (sense certainty, perception, and understanding) and transitions the reader to self-consciousness, he proceeds to describe six forms self-consciousness undergoes before arriving at the way of knowing described as reason—in which phrenology and physiognomy are criticized. These six forms of self-consciousness are Desire, One Self-Consciousness engaged in a life and death struggle against another Self-Consciousness, The Master-Slave Relationship, Stoicism, Skepticism, and the Unhappy Consciousness. It is by proceeding through these six forms of self-consciousness, that the self-conscious comes to realize what Reason is—particularly in the final form of self-consciousness, the Unhappy Consciousness. At the end of the section "Self-Consciousness," Hegel states that "in this object, in which it finds that its own action and being, as being that of this particular consciousness, are being and action in themselves, there has arisen for consciousness the idea of Reason, of the certainty that, in its particular individuality, it has being absolutely in itself, or is all reality."[2] In this section we will observe the development of one form of self-consciousness to another—beginning with Desire and ending with the Unhappy Consciousness. We will also analyze what Hegel means by "Reason" in the aforementioned quote, and what Hegel finds to be necessary to render a form of Self-Consciousness a form of Reason. Lastly, we will examine how Hegel understands Phrenology within the scope of his presentation on Reason as we proceed into the next section.

Hegel has transitioned the reader's attention away from the object, and toward the self through the realization that the absolute flux which the Understanding attributed to the structure of the object was, in fact, the structure and characteristic of the self-consciousness. Whenever the consciousness utilizes the Understanding to have knowledge of an object,

2. Hegel, *Phenomenology of Spirit*, 138.

what ends up being realized is that the Understanding is really only showing us the structure of the self-consciousness as it confronts objects in the world. In focusing now on the self-consciousness, Hegel acknowledges that the self-consciousness experiences desire or appetite for particular objects and this is because, as Hegel acknowledges, self-consciousness is a living thing. The self-consciousness seeks to satisfy its desire or appetite by consuming living things, but this satisfaction is only temporary, and the desire returns to the self-consciousness. For Hegel, this continued desire serves to demonstrate that although the object is consumed by the self-consciousness, and therefore experiences a unity with it—there remains a condition of independence which the object has from the self-consciousness, which is shown in the continued desire and satisfaction between self-consciousness and the object. Hegel describes this dilemma self-consciousness encounters, saying, "In this satisfaction, however, experience makes it aware that the object has its own independence. Desire and the self-certainty obtained in its gratification, are conditioned by the object, for self-certainty comes from superseding this other: in order that this supersession can take place, there must be this other."[3] Self-consciousness seeks unity between itself and the object, but the ongoing desire/appetite makes such unity impossible, and self-consciousness realizes that the unity it seeks is only possible in another self-consciousness. This encounter with another self-consciousness is what leads to the second form of self-consciousness, which is One Self-Consciousness engaged in a life and death struggle against another Self-Consciousness.

In the section entitled "Independence and Dependence of Self-consciousness: Lordship and Bondage," Hegel describes two self-consciousnesses encountering each other, and each seeking recognition in the other. Both self-consciousnesses understand themselves as more than just their particular self-consciousness, but rather they see their particular self-consciousness as equivalent to consciousness in general (because each sees itself as the only self-consciousness before the encounter with the other). The existence of a second self-consciousness, which is also particular and independent of the other self-consciousness provides an apparent contradiction for each self-consciousness and their understanding of self. It is because of this ostensible contradiction that a fight to the death ensues between the two self-consciousnesses. Each self-consciousness sees the other as an object. Hegel describes this interesting scene by explaining that

---

3. Hegel, *Phenomenology of Spirit*, 109.

"appearing thus immediately on the scene, they are for one another like ordinary objects, independent shapes, individuals submerged in the being [or immediacy] of Life—for the object in its immediacy is here determined as Life."[4] It is through this struggle to the death that each self-consciousness attempts to demonstrate to the other that they are not merely an object in its immediacy before the other, but rather an independent self-consciousness. During this struggle to the death, however, as one self-consciousness is about to die, it realizes that life is essential to its being, yields to the desire of the other self-consciousness, and in exchange for its life, agrees to be the servant of the other self-consciousness. It is through this agreement between the two self-consciousnesses that Hegel moves the reader from the second form of self-consciousness (One Self-Consciousness engaged in a life and death struggle against another Self-Consciousness) to the third form of self-consciousness (The Master-Slave Relationship).

Hegel describes this third form of self-consciousness, relating to two self-consciousnesses, as follows: "one is the independent consciousness whose essential nature is to be for itself, the other is the dependent consciousness whose essential nature is simply to live or to be for another. The former is lord, the other is bondsman."[5] In this form of self-consciousness the bondsman is allowed to live, but the bondsman essentially lives as a thing—a thing in which the master has power over. It is because the master has continued power over the servant, that the master receives the recognition that was originally sought in the first form of self-consciousness (i.e., Desire). The servant, in continually doing the will of the master both acknowledges the master as a consciousness that is for itself, while at the same time the servant acknowledges its existence as an object obedient to the will of the master. This arrangement, however, Hegel explains has the reverse effect, in that it demonstrates that the self-consciousness of the master is not independent, but rather is dependent on the recognition which the servant continually provides. Likewise, the self-consciousness of the servant is not dependent, but rather it is independent and for itself—and this can be seen in the work it does (for the master ostensibly) so that it can continue to have life. Hegel further elaborates on the essential nature of this life, which the servant seeks to preserve referring to it as "absolute negativity, pure being-for-self," which is discovered when the servant is faced with death.

---

4. Hegel, *Phenomenology of Spirit*, 113.
5. Hegel, *Phenomenology of Spirit*, 115.

The servant realizes its being is more important than the servitude that it continually performs through work for the master.

This realization that the servant's essential nature is being-in-itself-and-for-itself, which the servant discovers through work, moves the self-consciousness of the servant to the fourth form of self-consciousness, which Hegel explains to be stoicism. Work is defined by Hegel as "desire held in check,"[6] and it is through this work that the servant qua worker understands a correspondence between the independence of the object, and the independence of their own being. The object is shaped by the servant, and in the shaping of the object through work there is a correspondence between the essential nature of the servant and the object, that in its shaping reflects this essential nature. Concerning this fourth stage of self-consciousness, Hegel explains that "self-will is the freedom which entrenches itself in some particularity and is still in bondage, while Stoicism is the freedom which always comes directly out of bondage and returns into the pure universality of thought."[7] Stoicism is also the first form of self-consciousness which Hegel explicitly mentions has manifested itself in the history of thought, but the inadequacy of this form stems from the fact that it does not have particular content to draw upon to establish adequate criteria of what is true and good and reasonable. This is the case because stoicism, according to Hegel, propounds the principle that "consciousness is a being that thinks, and that consciousness holds something to be essentially important, or true and good only in so far as it thinks it to be such."[8] Hegel quickly shows how this fourth form of self-consciousness soon leads to the fifth form of self-consciousness, which is skepticism (here the form of skepticism which Hegel has in mind is mostly likely Pyrrhonian, but with its skeptical focus, dialectically speaking, being that of stoicism)—particularly skepticism over whether what stoicism, as a form of self-consciousness took to be true, is in fact true. Hegel explains that skepticism finds that it can just as easily doubt the very things that the prior form of self-consciousness posited to be the case—and this is because stoicism, according to Hegel had no "criterion of truth as such."

However, as skepticism proceeds to doubt all aspects of reality, it immediately experiences contradictions—contradictions which Hegel proposes can be best understood as an oscillation between two extremes. Hegel describes the contradictions in skepticism in its two extremes as

---

6. Hegel, *Phenomenology of Spirit*, 117–18.
7. Hegel, *Phenomenology of Spirit*, 121.
8. Hegel, *Phenomenology of Spirit*, 121.

what it asserts and what it is while it is asserting as much. Hegel finds that "It [skepticism] lets the unessential content in its thinking vanish; but just in doing so it is the consciousness of something unessential. It pronounces an absolute vanishing, but the pronouncement *is*, and this consciousness is the vanishing that is pronounced. It affirms the nullity of seeing, hearing, etc., yet it is itself seeing, hearing etc. . . . But it keeps the poles of this its self-contradiction apart, and adopts the same attitude to it as it does in its purely negative activity in general."[9] Although Hegel explains that skepticism keeps these two contradictory aspects of its self-consciousness apart—once these two self-contradictory aspects are brought together so that self-consciousness is aware of such a contradiction and oscillation (between a skeptical self-consciousness and a self-consciousness that contradicts itself by assuming the very ideas it is skeptical about), the final form of self-consciousness takes shape. Hegel refers to this sixth and final form of self-consciousness as the unhappy consciousness.

Hegel further utilizes the third form of consciousness, Lord and Bondsman, to describe the internal conflict and the contradictory nature of the unhappy consciousness. This unhappy consciousness observes the dual nature of itself as possessing both an unchangeable, essential nature as well as a changeable inessential nature—and the unhappy consciousness identifies with the changeable inessential nature. Hegel explains that a consequence of this identification is that the unhappy consciousness views the unchangeable nature as alien to itself. However, unity is attempted in this self-consciousness when individuality is linked to unchangeableness, and when each self-consciousness acknowledges the other self-consciousness as itself. Hegel explains that "through these two moments of reciprocal self-surrender of both parts, consciousness does, of course, gain a sense of its unity with the Unchangeable."[10] This ostensible solution that the unhappy consciousness experiences, however, is not permanent; the only way the individuality and the Unchangeable are able to be brought together is through the syllogistic understanding of a middle term. This particular middle term being a mediator, minister, or priest. Through renouncing everything and following the instructions of the mediator, this unhappy consciousness—according to Hegel—gives up its "I" and turns its consciousness into a thing, making it objective.

---

9. Hegel, *Phenomenology of Spirit*, 125.
10. Hegel, *Phenomenology of Spirit*, 134.

We come now to the final sentence Hegel writes in his section on self-consciousness before proceeding to reason, and the ideas in this sentence serve to elucidate the movement Hegel desires his readers to make from self-consciousness to reason. Hegel writes, "But in this object [mediator as counsellor], in which it finds that its own action and being, as being that of this particular consciousness, are being and action in themselves, there has arisen for consciousness the idea of Reason, of the certainty that, in its particular individuality, it has being absolutely in itself, or is all reality."[11] Reason (or the possibility of the self-consciousness obtaining reason) stems from the experience of the unhappy consciousness unifying its self-consciousness through obedience to a mediator, and with this there is a move to intersubjective agreement and experience of the "Unchangeable." This movement can be more comprehensively understood as the intersubjective agreement of what Reason is, i.e., it is the self-consciousness that the mediator provides. This existence of the mediator communicates the possibility to self-consciousness that Reason is something that both the Unchangeable and the individual self-consciousness can share—and if the self-consciousness can share in the knowledge of the Unchangeable then its knowledge will also be absolute in nature. The only thing left for Hegel to do now is to proceed to Reason—and take his reader on the path that reason must in fact take to align itself with the absolute. In the next section we will examine the path which Hegel explains that reason takes. What will be of specific importance for us is the difference Hegel marks between perception and observation, as well as how errors in reasoning such as those of Phrenology (as well as Physiognomy and Palmistry) fit into Hegel's overall presentation of Reason—and how such types of errors are ultimately overcome.

Hegel's Presentation of Phrenology
(as well as Physiognomy and Palmistry)

Quentin Lauer begins the sixth chapter of his commentary, *A Reading of Hegel's Phenomenology of Spirit* (which is his commentary on Hegel's chapter of Reason [chapter 5]) by saying, "When we approach Chapter 5 of Hegel's *Phenomenology*, we run the risk of becoming engulfed in a confusion out of which we shall not subsequently be able to extricate ourselves."[12]

---

11. Hegel, *Phenomenology of Spirit*, 138.
12. Lauer, *A Reading of Hegel's "Phenomenology of Spirit,"* 149.

Lauer's words are not incorrect. Hegel's chapter on Reason is divided into three sections, and each of these sections are divided into three subsections. The first of the three sections is entitled, "Observing Reason"; Hegel's discussion of Phrenology is found in the third subsection of this first section, which he refers to as "Observation of self-consciousness in its relation to its immediate actuality. Physiognomy and Phrenology." Hegel describes his goal for this chapter (and essentially for the remainder of the *Phenomenology of Spirit*) as being the observation of the process of consciousness becoming reason. Hegel explains that "Consciousness, however, as essence is this whole process itself, of passing out of itself as simple categories into a singular individual, into the object, and of contemplating this process in the object, nullifying the object as distinct [from it], appropriating it as its own, and proclaiming itself as this certainty of being all reality, of being both itself and itself object."[13] We are now in the phase of the *Phenomenology of Spirit* where Hegel has defined reason as "the certainty of being all reality" which he equates with idealism. But for Hegel it is one thing to assert this truth about reason and quite another thing to follow the path of reason until reason reaches the point where it asserts this truth from experience. This is why Hegel explains that "anyone who has not trodden this path [the path Hegel's *Phenomenology* is about to take beginning in chapter 5 "The Certainty and the Truth of Reason"] finds this assertion [i.e., "Reason is the certainty of consciousness that it is all reality"] incomprehensible when it hears it in this pure form."[14] We quickly come to Hegel's presentation of Phrenology along this path of reason, as an error of reason as we attempt to observe reason, first in nature, then through logical and psychological laws, and finally in relation to the particular physicality of human beings.

Hegel begins with observations of nature (as the first subsection), in which he attempts to observe reason in natural phenomena, including both organic and inorganic. Hegel finds that such objects contain both a universality and a particularity (when dealing with organic phenomena Hegel will also use the labels of species and genus to refer to his type of distinction), and that he cannot directly observe the universality in the object itself. Hegel utilizes many examples to elucidate this situation in which reason is not fully present in the object or that we can be mistaken as to how reason is present in the object. I find that Hegel's two most salient examples are that of the pen-knife and snuff and that of resin-electricity

13. Hegel, *Phenomenology of Spirit*, 144.
14. Hegel, *Phenomenology of Spirit*, 140.

and glass-electricity. The former example, for Hegel, being an example of the former situation, meaning the pen-knife and sniff demonstrate the situation in which reason is not fully present in the object, and the latter example, meaning the example of the resin-electricity and the glass-electricity being an example of the latter uncertainty that we have with respect to reason as we are observing natural objects. This latter uncertainty being understood as an uncertainty because it demonstrates that we are mistaken as to how reason is present in the object. With the example of the penknife and the snuff-box, Hegel explains, "What is perceived should at least have the significance of a universal, not of a senuous particular."[15] Hegel is initially attempting to demonstrate the difference between observing reason and mere perception. Given mere perception, one would not necessarily view an object or a thing per se, but instead, view merely a variety of sensuous particulars that may or may not be distinguished as an object such as a penknife or a snuff-box. With observing reason, however, we observe that these objects are in fact both particular objects as well as types of things. Reason can observe both the universality of the object and the particularity of the object. With observing reason, we acknowledge that the universality of the thing is not present in the various sensuous particulars of the thing—yet it is through reason that we observe both the concept and the precepts of a thing. Reason, according to Hegel, allows us to apprehend the universal within the precepts of particularity. With the latter example of resin electricity and glass electricity, Hegel shows how the particularity of resin and glass were mistakenly attached to the concept of electricity, when in fact the actuality of the concept of electricity involves an understanding of its concept in terms of positive and negative. Hegel explains that "negative electricity, which at first comes to be known, say as resin-electricity, and positive electricity as glass-electricity, these, as a result of experiments, lose altogether such a significance and become purely positive and negative electricity, neither of which is any longer attached to a particular kind of thing; and we can no longer say that there are bodies which are positively electrical and others which are negatively electrical."[16]

To further explicate what Hegel is attempting to distinguish with this latter example concerning an error in reason, it may be helpful to turn to a more salient example of such an error which Descartes' ideas appear to point out. Descartes had no reservations about reducing animals to

---

15. Hegel, *Phenomenology of Spirit*, 147.
16. Hegel, *Phenomenology of Spirit*, 153.

automata. This reduction led him to suppose that, for example, an actual flesh and blood cat would be by nature no different than an identical automaton of said cat. Whatever the nature of a cat is, it is not flesh and blood (this becomes obvious for Descartes once he imagines an automaton of a cat being rendered and imagining no significant difference between the biological cat and the automaton) but rather flesh and blood are accidental qualities of the cat and are not essential to the understanding of its nature. Hegel is explaining a similar situation involving electricity. It was mistakenly thought by reason that resin and glass were essential to the understanding of the nature of electricity, but these qualities associated with electricity were merely accidental, philosophically speaking. In this example we have the supposed universality of the concept of resin electricity and glass electricity, which reason, as opposed to perception, discovers to be positive and negative electricity instead—which it then takes to be essential to the concept of electricity.

Hegel acknowledges that when we observe nature we find the Notion in our recognition of the universality of the object observed, but that such universality exists in self-consciousness rather than in the object. With this realization Hegel directs the reader to focus on observing self-consciousness, and in particular observing the "Laws of Thought" which he finds to be both logical and psychological. Concerning the laws of logic, Hegel finds difficulty establishing their truth because if we are to abstract the laws from our observation of the object, we cannot be certain that the laws are true as particular laws. Let us take, for example, the object of salt, which is a favorite example for Hegel. Here the laws of thought may abstract a unity in this object among its many properties (e.g., whiteness, bitterness, cubical in shape). As we abstract this unity, Hegel indicates that it becomes unclear whether such a law of unity or determinateness belongs to the object as a law of it, or rather if such a law belongs to the laws of thought. Hegel indicates that the question becomes: Are these laws chiefly a product of the self-consciousness? Furthermore, when we observe the laws in our observation of the object, we do not view the laws as individual laws, but rather as expressed in the unity of the object. The laws as divided into individual laws appear only to exist in the self-consciousness and not in the object. This universality (of the individual laws) which is found to be in self-consciousness, Hegel claims can be seen both as the negative of the object as well as an actuality in itself.

Considering the self-consciousness now as an actuality in itself, Hegel directs the reader to the psychological laws that follow. Hegel explains that self-consciousness has both individuality and universal being, and he illustrates this with the example of wrong doing or crime. Hegel finds that the universal being (i.e., Spirit) conforms itself "to the habits, customs, and way of thinking already to hand,"[17] (Here Hegel may be alluding to his aforementioned ideas of the inverted world as well.) but that an opposition to such conformity within the individual can also take place in the form of crime or wrongdoing when the individual "sets aside that actuality in a merely individual manner, or when it does this in a general way and thus for all, putting another world, another right, law, and custom in place of those already existing."[18] Much like the individual who deviates from the laws and customs of the particular milieu, Hegel finds that observational psychology observes many faculties of the mind, moving in all directions and is "astonished that such a contingent medley of heterogeneous beings can be together in the mind like things in a bag, more especially since they show themselves to be not dead, inert things but restless movements."[19] Furthermore, each individual appears to be a particular combination of this unity and this "contingent medley," and when Hegel inquires into where the particularity of each individual comes from—i.e., from either the "essential nature of the universal Spirit" or from the "contingent particularization"—it appears that the rules of psychology are at a loss or rather they experience a contradiction. These laws experience a contradiction because it appears that both aforementioned aspects are what constitute the laws of psychology.

Both aforementioned aspects are quite different, and yet Hegel finds that the laws of psychology are established from both the inorganic nature as well as the individuality. Hegel compares this situation to that of a "double gallery of pictures" which he then explains by the interesting phrase, "the one, the gallery of external circumstances which completely determine and circumscribe the individual, the other, the same gallery translated into the form in which those circumstances are present in the conscious individual: the former the spherical surface, the latter the centre which represents that surface within it."[20] For Hegel, this situation, which

17. Hegel, *Phenomenology of Spirit*, 182.
18. Hegel, *Phenomenology of Spirit*, 182.
19. Hegel, *Phenomenology of Spirit*, 182.
20. Hegel, *Phenomenology of Spirit*, 183.

the "double gallery of pictures" represents, renders psychological necessity, and therefore psychological laws, meaningless because in this double gallery of sorts, freedom and necessity appear indistinguishable. Demonstrating this contradiction, Hegel moves the reader to an examination of phrenology and physiognomy to pursue an observation of the attempt to attach psychological laws to individual actuality.

Hegel begins this examination of phrenology and physiognomy (as well as palmistry) in the third part of this first section which he entitles, "Observation of the Relation of Self-Consciousness to its Immediate Actuality. Physiognomy and Phrenology." By "immediate actuality," Hegel means "the body of the specific individuality" and so the task of this section is to examine systems of thought which relate (in a law-like fashion) the self-consciousness of an individual to their particular body. The systems which do this, or, at least purport to do this, according to Hegel, include palmistry, physiognomy, and phrenology. Hegel is specific in his argument that it is an arbitrary shape of the body as opposed to an organ of the body or an activity of the body, and this is because an organ such as the organ of speech, or an action such as the action of walking, can misrepresent the intentions of the self-consciousness. Such misrepresentations of the self-consciousness can intentionally be done by the self-consciousness, or it can be unintentional—but either way, Hegel claims that we cannot rely on either organs or activity as a reliable indicator of the inner activity of self-consciousness. Instead, Hegel explores the possibility of the arbitrary shape of the body providing such access to the inner state of self-consciousnesses, explaining, "If now the outer shape could express the inner individuality only in so far as that shape is neither an organ nor an action, hence only in so far as it is a passive whole, it would behave as an existent Thing, which passively received the inner as an alien element into its passive existence, and thereby became a sign of it—an external contingent expression whose actual aspect lacked any meaning of its own."[21]

Hegel first explores this possibility in the case of physiognomy, and immediately contrasts physiognomy with palmistry and astrology (the latter are different for Hegel because they associate "only an outer to an outer," meaning, they simply associate two external factors with each other). Hegel soon reconsiders whether palmistry is simply associating two external factors (a person's fate and the lines on their hands). He reexamines the idea of fate as an internal factor and states, "For fate itself is also only the manifestation

21. Hegel, *Phenomenology of Spirit*, 188.

of what the particular individuality is *in itself* as an inner original specific character."[22] Hegel, therefore, finds palmistry to be akin to physiognomy in this way, and attempts to provide some rationale as to why the hand would be associated with fate, explaining, "We may say of the hand that it *is* what the man *does*, for in its, as the active organ of his self-fulfillment, he is present as the animating soul; and since he is primarily his own fate, his hand will thus express his in-itself."[23] Hegel then provides a similar rationale for the face before engaging in the topic of physiognomy. Again, however, because the particular actions of the organ of the hand or the expressions of the face can be intentionally misleading, or unintentionally inaccurate of the individual's inner state, Hegel designates such actions or expressions as inessential, and explains that physiognomy finds instead the outer shape of the face to be an essential expression of the individual's inner character, or "presumed [outward] presence of Spirit."[24]

Hegel comes out very strongly against physiognomy, describing it in two very different ways. He describes physiognomy as a critic, which is the way he in fact sees it, saying that "the *laws* which this 'science' sets out to find are relations between these two supposed aspects, and hence can themselves be nothing more than empty subjective opinions.... As regards their content [the observations of physiognomy], however, these observations are on a par with these: 'It always rains when we have our annual fair,' says the dealer; 'and every time, too,' says the housewife, 'when I am drying my washing.'"[25] Hegel conversely provides an interesting description of physiognomy from the point of view of the individual who subscribes to it saying "True, it [the opinion of the individual who believes the claims of physiognomy] is also just this reflectedness into itself, out of sense, in sensuous form, and this which is visibly present as visibility of the invisible,

---

22. Hegel, *Phenomenology of Spirit*, 188.

23. Hegel, *Phenomenology of Spirit*, 189.

24. Although phrenology is at present understood as a pseudoscience, during Hegel's time it was widely accepted as a legitimate source of knowledge. Quoting Judith Shklar, Verene encourages the reader to understand that during the time of Hegel, phrenology was not understood as a pseudoscience: "This 'science' was generally accepted by the most advanced opinion for decades after Hegel wrote. This was no straw man. One need only recall the influence of Cesare Lombroso on criminology to recognize how important a part measuring skulls played in the development of the social sciences. It was Lombroso's belief that by measuring the skulls of prisoners one would determine who was, and by implication who was not, a criminal type. Traces of this sort of reasoning are, in fact, by no means extinct now." Verene, *Hegel's Recollection*, 81.

25. Hegel, *Phenomenology of Spirit*, 193.

is the object of observation. But just this sensuous immediate presence is the *reality* of Spirit only for mere opinion."[26] Given both of these descriptions we find that Hegel understands such conclusions of physiognomy to be nothing more than "empty subjective opinions," whereas for the individuals who subscribe to those opinions Hegel correctly expresses that they falsely believe the empirically visible particular features of the face indicate the invisible characteristics of the particular self-consciousness. Protesting the conclusions of physiognomy, Hegel essentially rejects the latter premise, which the physiognomist subscribes to in preference to the idea that action is the true being of the individual, saying "The *true being* of a man is rather his deed."[27] This statement appears to dismiss the very premises that these types of pseudosciences are based on, but before Hegel does dismiss these forms of reasoning in favor of "The actualization of rational self-consciousness through its own activity," Hegel explores and rejects phrenology.

Hegel examines phrenology in like manner to his examinations of palmistry and physiognomy, by first providing some rationale for the particular location of the body being utilized, and then by supplying a comparison in which the absurdity of the system of thought can be recognized. Hegel explains that the skull appears to be utilized because of its close proximity to the brain—the brain being understood to be the organ most directly related to self-consciousness. Hegel understands phrenology to claim that either the shape of the skull affects or indicates activity of the self-consciousness, or vice versa. In reality Hegel finds that any connections or observations made by this system of thought would be arbitrary in nature. Furthermore, Hegel provides an interesting analogy to show the absurdity of the project of phrenology; this analogy involves the children of Israel identifying themselves with the sands of the seashore. In this analogy Hegel explains, "If the children of Israel, who were likened in number to the sands of the sea-shore, should each take unto himself the grain of sand which stood for him, the indifference and arbitrariness of such a procedure would be no more glaring than that which assigns to every faculty of soul, to every passion, and—what must equally be considered here—to each nuance of character which the more refined psychology and 'knowledge of human nature' likes to talk about, its particular area of skull and shape of skull-bone."[28]

26. Hegel, *Phenomenology of Spirit*, 192.
27. Hegel, *Phenomenology of Spirit*, 194.
28. Hegel, *Phenomenology of Spirit*, 202.

After providing this tantamount absurdity to what he finds the insights of phrenology to amount to, Hegel again draws on his former comparison concerning individuals who link (in some supposed law-like fashion) rainy weather to activities and actions that do not go well with rain. This time, however, when revisiting this former comparison with phrenology in mind, Hegel address the phenomenon of what "ought to be present," which provides the groundwork for a contradiction of what reason is. Reason, for Hegel, being that a claim cannot be proven by both x and ~x; such as if x then y, and if x then ~y. Hegel explains that for example when the annual fair occurs or when a person begins to hang their wash (both supposed indications of rain) and if it does not rain that these individual might say "that *really* it *ought* to rain, and that the *tendency* to rain is certainly *present*."[29] Further commenting on such ideas of what "ought to be present," Hegel states, "but if the *reality* is not present, the *empty possibility* serves equally well."[30] And here if we understand the reality to be "x," then the empty possibility would be understood as "~x." After providing the example, Hegel then argues that an analogous inductive fallacy occurs in the observations of phrenology because phrenology allows for particular claims about particular self-consciousnesses to be drawn from the particular shape of particular skulls, while at the same time it also allows for the opposite claim to be drawn from the same evidence (here Hegel is essentially claiming the phrenologist is utilizing tactics similar to the "No True Scotsman" fallacy)—and this Hegel finds is the very opposite (or perhaps inversion) of reason, explaining, "We see mere subjective imagining brought by the very nature of the fact to say—but *unthinkingly*—the opposite of what it affirms; to say that by this particular bone something or other is indicated, but equally too, is *not* indicated."[31]

For Hegel phrenology is the opposite of reason because of this evident propensity for contradiction (which was formerly mentioned), and Hegel suggests that the reader move in the very opposite direction, reversing course in the path of observation which they have been travelling down in pursuit of comprehending the phrase that reason is the certainty of being all reality. Hegel suggests that the reader return to the first phase of reason, that of the observation of reason in inorganic life—and now instead of proceeding down the same path again which ended in the absurdity of

---

29. Hegel, *Phenomenology of Spirit*, 204.
30. Hegel, *Phenomenology of Spirit*, 204.
31. Hegel, *Phenomenology of Spirit*, 204.

phrenology, to confirm rather the truth of this statement that reason is present in inorganic life.[32] After going through this process of returning to the first phase of reason, Hegel asserts that the reader can now understand that the universal is present not only in self-consciousness, but in the object as well; this process of realization is what Hegel refers to as "unitary being." The self-consciousness can also recognize through reason, itself as the Notion, which is Spirit, and observes its own essence as the universality which is Spirit. Reason now grasps Spirit in the object, i.e., in the various movements of consciousness. Spirit is not the content of these moments any more than it is the contents of a skull-bone, but rather reason acknowledges that the contents of such moments point to Spirit. Hegel finds that the reader can observe each moment as a moment of Spirit. The reader, according to Hegel, understands the movement of reason to be Spirit aiming to manifest itself in the reason of the individual who observes it. The reader now understands what reason is not and must move in the opposite direction. Hegel explains this insight involving the reversal of the idea of phrenology and the return to the starting point of inorganic nature in the following way, "What was ruled out by the very first observation of inorganic Nature, viz. the idea that the Notion ought to be present in the form of a Thing, is reinstated by this last form of observation in such a way that it turns the reality of Spirit itself into a Thing or, expressing it the other way round, gives to lifeless being the significance of Spirit."[33] One has now seen the error of making Spirit a "lifeless being" and must return to the beginning, positing Spirit to be present in inorganic nature.

Before we examine how Hegel's Presentation of Phrenology can relate to it being understood as a Pseudoscience, we will briefly examine how this conclusion at the end of this section of Hegel's chapter on "The Certainty and Truth of Reason" relates to the other two sections of this chapter (i.e., "The actualization of rational self-consciousness through its own activity" and "Individuality which takes itself to be real in and for itself"). After establishing that Spirit is present in the object, Hegel directs the reader to a "twofold significance" of this realization. We examine the first significance

32. Here Hegel explains, "But Reason, in its role of observer, having reached thus far, seems also to have reached its peak, at which point it must abandon itself and do a right-about turn; for only what is wholly bad is implicitly charged with the immediate necessity of changing round into its opposite.... Thus it is that this final stage of Reason in its observational role is its worst; and that is why its reversal becomes a necessity." Hegel, *Phenomenology of Spirit*, 206.

33. Hegel, *Phenomenology of Spirit*, 208.

which directly relates to the transition to the next section, "The actualization of Rational Self-Consciousness through its own Activity," due to its focus on the necessity of activity. The first significance is that self-consciousness realizes that it is "the immediate unity of being and self," but that to have knowledge or judgment of what exists (what Hegel refers to as "infinite judgment"), this unity between being and self has to be mediated by self-consciousness. This means, according to Hegel, that the activity of self-consciousness should not be spent examining the object, per se, but rather should be to "produce itself by its own activity." How to "produce itself by its own activity" becomes the focus of the next section.

Now reason must be found in human activity, in which Hegel directs the reader to explore three such activities—all three of which ultimately prove contradictory. The first of these activities is discussed under the title, "Pleasure and Necessity," in which one seeks one's own desire as a way of experiencing individuality, but one soon becomes a slave to this pursuit and a victim of fate because one is merely pursuing whatever one finds immediately pleasurable. The second of these activities is discussed under the title "The law of the heart and the frenzy of self-conceit"; here Hegel explains that one decides to impose on all others what they find to be the best for society and they impose this "law of the heart" universally, making an arbitrary sentiment into a universal law. This activity, however, breaks down because it is not based on universal reason, but rather on arbitrary sentiment—this also leads to insanity in the individual advocating an arbitrary sentiment as a universal law (though it is unclear if Hegel thinks that insanity is always the necessary outcome of such circumstances). The third activity which Hegel then instructs the reader to examine is under the title, "Virtue and the Way of the World." Here the reader explores virtue, but it is soon realized that the abstract notion of virtue is, in itself, powerless to produce virtuous action—and therefore the production of virtuous action is contingent on what Hegel calls the "course of events."

Since Hegel finds that virtue is not what is ultimately behind human action, he turns to individuality and explores the possibility concerning whether individuality is ultimately behind human action. Hegel does this in the third section of Reason, entitled, "Individuality which takes itself to be real in and for itself," and he investigates how human action relates to human spirit in the first subsection, which he refers to as "the spiritual animal kingdom and deceit, or the 'matter in hand' itself." If it is individuality which takes itself to be real, Hegel wishes to examine the activity which brings about this reality—particularly he wishes to show the reader how it is that self-consciousness, which is an individual self-consciousness, understands what it is to be an individual. This first part of the title, i.e., "the spiritual animal kingdom," refers to the belief Hegel holds that humans are not simply natural beings, but are spiritual beings as well. By "spiritual" Hegel does not mean anything remotely like the dualism of Descartes, but rather he means that we have activities or goals that develop us into who we are as individuals.[34] This activity is what Hegel refers to as the "matter in hand." The "matter in hand," is the spiritual activity which the individual engages in so that it may learn both what it is as an individual, and that it is more than just natural being. The "deceit" is experienced when an individual believes they are engaging in the activity for the stated goal of the activity, as opposed to the stated goal of understanding individuality through the activity of Spirit.[35] Once the self-consciousness realizes this it understands that this is the truth of all individuals, and therefore, it experiences a fusion of individuality and universality. In further exploration of this connection experienced between individuality and universality, Hegel turns to the moral law which is universal for the sake of the individual.

Hegel first examines "Reason as law giver," primarily by examining two laws (commandments) which are taken to be universal—e.g., one should always tell the truth, and love thy neighbor as thyself—but upon further examination,[36] Hegel shows that these laws are not universal but

---

34. Here Lauer explains that "the distinction which Hegel is making, however, is between *activities*—"spiritual" and "natural"—which distinction does not require distinct *substantial* sources of the activities." Lauer, *A Reading of Hegel's "Phenomenology of Spirit,"* 192.

35. Commenting on this idea, Lauer gives the example of the scholar (because he finds that the context Hegel has in mind is the "'intellectual' community." Here Lauer writes, "What the individual gives out as purely disinterested objectivity turns out to be pure self-interest. The scholar, for example, whose only interest is 'that the truth may appear' turns out to be concerned only that *his* truth may appear, or that *he* be the one who makes it appear. But he also deceives himself; his emphasis on the *his* of 'his affair' cannot cancel out the universality of 'what really matters.' . . . What it all comes down to in the context—and the context seems to be that of the 'intellectual' community (*das geistige Tierreich*)—is that anyone who *does* anything significant will soon find others flocking to do the same, not because of 'objective' interest but because each wants it to be his own doing." It is quite fascinating that Hegel conceptualizes human intellectual activity in this way (if Lauer's comments are indeed correct) given his philosophical enterprise. Lauer, *A Reading of Hegel's "Phenomenology of Spirit,"* 196

36. Hegel finds that a law such as one should always tell the truth is a contradictory statement for the following reasons: That it is contingent on the fact that one knows the

contradictory, because while claiming to be universal, they are in fact contingent (*Pace* Kant). Hegel then moves to an examination of "Reason as testing laws," which is the last section on Reason before Spirit. Hegel transitions from the former activity of reason to the latter because he finds he has shown that reason cannot provide laws that are universal, but instead when it attempts to it only contradicts itself. What this shows to Hegel, however, is that although reason cannot provide a universal law, it knows what the criteria are for a law to be universal—and with this new insight in mind Hegel proceeds to "Reason as testing laws."

In this last section, Hegel examines whether a suitable test of a law is that it is not self-contradictory; however this appears an unsatisfactory criteria because both a claim and the opposite of the claim can be universalized—and Hegel demonstrates this with the example of whether there should be property. Hegel further provides an additional example concerning a person being entrusted with another's property, but then changing their mind concerning what the idea of property is, so that the idea of "property" would no longer apply. Hegel finds that such an action is wrong but that the wrongness of the action has nothing to do with whether or not it is self-contradictory. Commenting on the aforementioned situation, Hegel explains, "It is not, therefore, because I find something is not self-contradictory that it is right; on the contrary, it is right because it is what is right [para. 437]."[37] Hegel also finds that when one acknowledges this "absoluteness of right" one is "within the ethical structure," which is the "essence of self-consciousness"—and with this final insight, Hegel moves to the topic of Spirit.

How Hegel's Presentation of Phrenology Relates to Phrenology Being Understood as a Pseudoscience

In the remaining sections we examine how Hegel's presentation of phrenology relates to phrenology being understood as a pseudoscience. We

---

truth, and that one is able to provide reassurance to oneself that one does in fact know the truth. Explaining how this contradicts the former law that one should always tell the truth, Hegel states, "For speaking the truth is made contingent on whether I can know it, and can convince myself of it; and the proposition says nothing more than that a confused muddle of truth and falsehood ought to be spoken just as anyone happens to know, mean or understand it." Hegel demonstrates similar contradictions with the law that one should love thy neighbor as thyself. Hegel, *Phenomenology of Spirit*, 254.

37. Hegel, *Phenomenology of Spirit*, 261–62.

do so as a means of investigating the second skeptical discovery, which is that coherence epistemologies allow the absurd (again note: "the absurd" is only considered absurd to those who do not subscribe to the particular epistemology) to become a historical reality, in which Hegel sees phrenology as a prime example of such an absurdity in history. When exploring the implications of Hegel's presentation of phrenology we will draw upon the work of Alasdair MacIntyre and David Verene. Although almost no one today would hesitate to label phrenology a pseudoscience—both of these authors caution thinking about phrenology as a pseudoscience during the time of Hegel.[38] These authors also seek broader comparison with phrenology and contemporary sciences—and it is these aspects of their comments that we will be examining more closely.

In his article "Hegel on Faces and Skulls," MacIntyre (after explaining Hegel's arguments against physiognomy and phrenology) shares his insight concerning a particular contemporary thesis. MacIntyre's insight involves "the thesis that there are biochemical or neural states of affairs, processes, and events, the occurrence and the nature of which are sufficient causes of human actions," and MacIntyre explains that "this thesis wore phrenological clothing in 1807; today its clothing is as fashionable as it was then, only the fashions are not what they were."[39] MacIntyre finds that Hegel's argument against phrenology would also be an argument against contemporary scientific fields which operate with this thesis relating to mind. This is to say that although MacIntyre is aware of phrenology's lack of falsifiability as well as the post hoc reasoning that Hegel compares it to, he finds that what Hegel disagrees with most is the type of explanation being supplied by phrenology. After providing some examples from Hegel as well as an example of his own (which we will consider in a moment), MacIntyre provides an additional example—a generalized example involving a belief in witchcraft to supply an ostensibly more prominent distinction concerning how the way the word "explain" can be understood quite differently. This distinction MacIntyre finds identifies what is most objectionable to Hegel concerning the "explanations" provided by phrenology.

In the example involving a belief in witchcraft MacIntyre explains, "Some Africans who believe in witchcraft point out that to explain the onset of a disease by referring to bacterial or virus infection leaves unexplained such facts as that Jones should have been afflicted by an infection

---

38. See 11nn13–14 above.
39. MacIntyre, "Hegel on Faces and Skulls," 225.

immediately after quarreling with Smith. "What is the cause of that conjunction?" they inquire, pointing out that Western science gives no answer."[40] The analogous connection which MacIntyre wants his readers to make between the unsatisfactory explanation (or lack of explanation) that believers in witchcraft find with the explanations provided by contemporary science concerning disease, and the unsatisfactory explanation (or lack of explanation) that Hegel finds with the explanation of phrenology concerning human nature is that certain causal relationships will not provide us with answers to other phenomena if it is not deemed by the system of reason to be related causally—and so not deemed worthy of attention when explaining the significance of a particular event. In the case of phrenology, Hegel claims, (according to MacIntyre) that it cannot provide us with any insight into rational human activity—even if it were a science and not a pseudoscience. It is this aforementioned point that MacIntyre wishes to stress with this analogous situation of believers in witchcraft. In the example of witchcraft we are able to readily understand that the reason contemporary science cannot provide the believer in witchcraft with the explanation for the causal relationship which they want explained has nothing to do with whether or not the science is a legitimate science (as opposed to a pseudoscience)[41] and has everything to do with the fact that the science does not share the same coherent framework of knowledge that the believers in witchcraft share (with respect to all the relevant factors requiring explanation when illness follows quarrelling). With this greater criticism of phrenology in mind (not the valid criticism that it is a pseudoscience), i.e., the criticism that it is unable to explain the rational activity of the self-consciousness, let us turn to the other examples of such inadequacies that MacIntyre provides.

Elaborating on the example Hegel provides of the murderer, MacIntyre aims to show first that Hegel believes "Traits are neither determinate nor fixed"[42] and that "a particular historical situation cannot on Hegel's view be dissolved into a set of properties."[43] MacIntyre demonstrates these ideas of Hegel's by expanding the example of the murderer to include the idea of

40. MacIntyre, "Hegel on Faces and Skulls," 231.

41. This is why MacIntyre cautions against viewing phrenology immediately as a pseudoscience in relation to Hegel's criticism—it is because he finds that one might miss Hegel's ultimate point in attacking phrenology. That point being that phrenology by its generalizations is unable to explain rational human activity.

42. MacIntyre, "Hegel on Faces and Skulls," 227.

43. MacIntyre, "Hegel on Faces and Skulls," 229.

dispositions in it. Here MacIntyre explains that "A given murderer, for instance, commits his crime because he fears his own humiliation by losing his beloved. If we are to look at the traits and other qualities manifested in his action, they do not include a disposition to commit murder, but such things perhaps as a general intolerance of suffering, a disposition to avoid specific kinds of humiliation, his love for the girl, and so on. The same disposition might explain to precisely the same extent the same person's outbidding others in giving to a deserving cause in order to impress the same girl. But just this fact puts in question the use of the word 'explain.'"[44] From MacIntyre's example we can come to appreciate why Hegel may claim that there is not a disposition to murder nor a disposition to be charitable, but only perhaps more general dispositions interacting with particular historical situations that results in behavior which is impossible to understand the cause of without accounting for the particular historical situation. MacIntyre also appears to think that the empiricist would disagree with such aforementioned beliefs—beliefs which are central to Hegel's thought—and claim rather that events are in fact reducible to a set of properties and that such properties are generalizable and applicable to a variety of situations despite the historical particularity of those situations.[45] MacIntyre, here is saying that if the historical particularity was taken into account when these sciences are making generalizations about particular sets of properties, then they would not be able to provide adequate explanations for their generalizations. This latter thesis, according to MacIntyre, is the underlying logic which produced the claims of phrenology during the time of Hegel, and produces similar theses in our contemporary sciences today—i.e., neurophysiology and genetics. Consequently, MacIntyre does not simply see Hegelianism as incompatible with the claims of phrenology (as Hegel himself did), but also as incompatible with such contemporary sciences as neurophysiology and genetics—to the extent that they hold this underlying thesis.[46] This thesis being that human

44. MacIntyre, "Hegel on Faces and Skulls," 228.

45. According to MacIntyre, the aforementioned empiricist thesis appears to be the opposite of what Hegel finds to be the case—explaining as much MacIntyre writes, "A murderer did not strike out at anyone who happened to have such and such properties but at this person. Just because this concreteness is not constituted by a mere collection of properties, it evades causal generalizations and so makes causal explanation, whether phrenological or neurophysiological, inapplicable." MacIntyre, "Hegel on Faces and Skulls," 231.

46. Here MacIntyre writes, "Whatever else the argument in this paper may or may not establish, they do seem to show that between the Hegelian mode of understanding human action and the mode that has dominated modern thinking about the relevance

behavior is both explainable and generalizable without considering the historical particularity of a situation.

Donald Verene in his chapter entitled "Phrenology," found in his work *Hegel's Recollection: A study of images in the Phenomenology of Spirit*, acknowledges MacIntyre's contribution to the understanding of Hegel's lengthy attack on phrenology, and both continues and elaborates on MacIntyre's point. Concerning MacIntyre's point that the thesis which was responsible for phrenology is now inhabiting such contemporary sciences as neurophysiology and genetics,[47] Verene finds this statement to be cogent, but selects behavioral psychology (particularly the behavioral psychology of B. F. Skinner) to compare to phrenology and physiognomy. Verene explains, "Were Hegel writing today he might just as well here refer to B. F. Skinner. . . . The difference between Skinner and Lavater or, later, Gall is that Skinner has done away with the inner entirely. The thesis of Skinner's popular book, *Beyond Freedom and Dignity*, is that freedom and dignity are not secret, inner motivations of individuals, but elements of behavior capable of observation. Like Skinner's thesis, Lavater's and Gall's also have a practical dimension. We can predict or divine behavior, and it follows that if we can do this we can alter behavior and character or in some way come to terms with it."[48] Verene further questions whether there is truly a distinction between phrenology and physiognomy on the one hand and the behavioral science of B. F. Skinner on the other, stating, "One might be tempted to say that there must be some difference between Skinner and such exponents of pseudo-science [meaning Lavater and Gall]"[49] and yet throughout the rest of Verene's examination of such a comparison he offers no such difference.[50]

Verene continues to compare and at times equate the thesis of behaviorism with the thesis of phrenology, and he argues that both systems of

---

of such sciences as neurophysiology and genetics, there is a basic incompatibility." MacIntyre, "Hegel on Faces and Skulls," 233–34.

47. See 11n13 above.

48. Verene, *Hegel's Recollection*, 83.

49. Verene, *Hegel's Recollection*, 83.

50. Furthermore, Verene continues this comparison, as opposed to providing any critical difference explaining that "Skinner is a controversial but respected figure in the profession of psychology. This is to forget that both Lavater and Gall were quite famous. Gall was a favorite of European aristocracy. Metternich, the Austrian prince and statesmen, thought him the greatest mind he had ever known; after his death Gall was mourned as a great pioneer scientist." Verene, *Hegel's Recollection*, 83.

thought can also be understood as being forms of "philosophical psychology, meaning that both behaviorism and phrenology seek to overcome a concept of the mind that is "inner," as opposed to empirically observable. Verene continues to explain this comparison, saying, "The instinct that philosophical psychology has followed is to get rid of the notion of mind as 'inner.' . . . To this point I have tried to emphasize that Hegel is refuting not simply pseudo-science in this section but also those doctrines of psychological science that attempt to observe mind and those philosophies of mind that are caught in the inner and outer distinction concerning mind."[51] Verene, then provides a final insight concerning Hegel's attack on phrenology, which is that he believes Hegel understands phrenology to be the inverse or upside-down version of phenomenology.[52] In asserting that Hegel finds phrenology to be the inverse of phenomenology, he also believes Hegel is making reference to the topsy-turvy world, which Hegel formerly mentioned in the section entitled "Force and Understanding."[53] What is different with this comparison is that there is no fundamental distinction (such as the phenomena/noumena distinction) between two worlds (e.g., one world where something is black and another world where the same thing is white, etc.) but rather, both of these systems of thought are existing in the same world.

What causes both of these systems of thought to exist (according to both Verene and MacIntyre) are differing theses concerning how to understand the activity of the rational self-consciousness. For Verene these two theses are not just different, they are opposite, and for MacIntyre, although Hegel reduced the particular ideas of phrenology to absurdity, the underlying thesis is still alive and well in certain contemporary sciences. And therefore, according to MacIntyre's interpretation of Hegel, these sciences would be treated by Hegel as equally absurd when they attempted to explain human action. At the very least, MacIntyre sees Hegelian phenomenology

51. Verene, *Hegel's Recollection*, 86–87.

52. Here Verene describes Phrenology as the upside-down version of phenomenology explaining that "Phrenology must be attacked so strongly, as an illusion of consciousness in its road to self-knowledge, not simply because it is a pseudo-science and represents bad thinking, but because it is the natural opposite, the inversion of the true science of mind—phenomenology." Verene, *Hegel's Recollection*, 89.

53. Here Verene explains that "in this passage (340) Hegel is playing on the topsy-turvy world metaphor. The immediate somersault that reason must accomplish is the manifestation of the self through its own activity. But Hegel's statements here have a wider significance. Phrenology is the upside-down of phenomenology." Verene, *Hegel's Recollection*, 90.

as profoundly incompatible with these contemporary sciences because of Hegel's emphasis on history when understanding self-consciousness. Given the comparative example which Verene provides between behaviorism and phrenology, he does not appear to make the case that there is a significant difference of kind between the particular science of behaviorism and the pseudoscience of phrenology. MacIntyre appears to make a distinction between the legitimate sciences of genetics and neurophysiology on the one hand and physiognomy and phrenology on the other—but he does not find this difference relevant to the argument which Hegel is making. This is because of MacIntyre's idea that the thesis behind phrenology can inhabit contemporary scientific forms.

We have so far examined ideas which show that phrenology is connected to an underlying thesis—that this thesis can inhabit both scientific and pseudoscientific reasoning—and that this thesis is the inverse of the thesis behind phenomenology. We have yet to explore how such ideas are connected to coherence epistemologies or how coherence epistemologies allow such forms of reasoning as phrenology to come into being. We will now turn to an examination of how coherence epistemologies allow forms of reasoning such as phrenology to come into being—i.e., become a historical reality.

Reason and Pseudoscience: A Difference of Degree Not Kind

Before we examine how coherence epistemologies allow systems of reason such as phrenology to become a historical reality, let us examine what we should understand a coherence epistemology to be. By the term "coherence epistemology" what is essentially meant is a Quinean conception of a web of knowledge—but with an emphasis on one important detail which Quine provides toward the end of his essay "Two Dogmas of Empiricism." Near the end of this essay, Quine describes one aspect of this web of knowledge by explaining that "Any statement can be held true come what may, if we make drastic enough adjustments elsewhere in the system. Even a statement very close to the periphery can be held true in the face of recalcitrant experience by pleading hallucination or by amending certain statements of the kind called logical laws."[54] Here Quine explains that although a web of knowledge relies upon a vast variety of truths that are interconnected and internally coherent, a particular statement can be held to be true no

---

54. Quine, "Two Dogmas of Empiricism," 20–43.

matter what (even though any statement is potentially subject to change). This is to say that any statement within the web of beliefs can be held to be absolute truth (truth which is dependent on nothing else but itself to be true) and this is somewhat ironic given that a web of knowledge requires coherence with other truths for a statement to be considered true. Quine, however, with this aforementioned statement, is claiming just the opposite of this concerning a statement held to be true, "come what may." However, we should note that this detail about a web of knowledge which Quine describes is not so much the essence of what a coherence epistemology is conceptually (or for that matter practically), nor is it conceptually what Quine has in mind when he further describes such a web of knowledge in his work *Web of Belief*—far from it.[55] Rather this detail concerning the Quinean web of knowledge is more of the Achilles heel of coherence epistemologies, one that if exploited drastically enough demonstrates the concern that a coherence epistemology can be internally coherent, while at the same time providing no correspondence with actuality.[56] What Quine's claim suggests is that a web of knowledge (coherence epistemology) has the potential to accommodate the following situation: A statement is arbitrarily created and designated to be absolute truth. This statement is then placed in the web of knowledge (Let us imagine that the arbitrary statement which was given the weight of absolute truth is "The universe and everything in it was created five minutes ago.") Quine's statement suggests that in this situation the web of knowledge is able to rearrange itself so that no matter how unbelievable a statement may appear, it can be accommodated by the coherence epistemology due to the fact that this web of knowledge is able to rearrange itself without limit (It is somewhat unclear what would make a claim absolute i.e., unable to be challenged for a time, so that facts which might challenge it are either ignored or reinterpreted in such a way that they do not challenge the belief, but instead support it in the mind of the individual holding the belief).

---

55. In his work *Web of Belief* Quine explains that "our adjustment of an inconsistent set of beliefs may be either decisive or indecisive. If it is decisive, each belief of the set is either kept or switched to disbelief. If it is indecisive, some beliefs simply give way to non-belief; judgement on them is suspended." Quine is here providing a description concerning how a web of beliefs should function, as opposed to the aforementioned detail he provides in the "Two Dogmas of Empiricism" which explains how a web of beliefs has the potential to also function. Quine, *Web of Belief*, 19.

56. For a description of these criticisms see Olsson, "Coherentism," 257–67.

Although this particular feature of the web of knowledge is articulated by Quine, Hegel does appear to indicate that he is aware of this feature of human reasoning when he is criticizing phrenology. Recall Hegel's earlier comparison of phrenology to the reasoning of the dealer or the midwife who explains that "*really* it *ought* to rain, and that the *tendency* to rain is certainly *present*."[57] Hegel is noting such reasoning provided by these individuals after the claim they made that it always will rain on wash-day or during the annual fair. This claim is made by both the dealer and the midwife, according to Hegel, when it has failed to rain on such days. This claim can be seen as aimed at preserving the former claim, i.e., that it always rains on wash-day or during the annual fair. If we look at these two claims as exemplifying the aforementioned aspect of the web of knowledge which Quine describes, i.e., "Any statement can be held true come what may," we see that the latter statement ("the tendency to rain is certainly present") is provided to ensure that the former statement (it will always rain on wash-day or during the annual fair) remains true even when confronted by contrary empirical evidence, i.e., that it did not rain on such a day. The question of why a particular claim should continue to be held to be true even in the presences of contrary evidence is not addressed by Hegel (nor does Quine provide an explanation concerning why anyone would want to hold a statement to be true "come what may"). The point is only that coherence epistemologies provide the structure which allows any statement to be held to be absolute truth (again coherence epistemologies only provide the structure—it is unclear where the motivation for such a tendency would originate—though custom and habit no doubt play a role), if one is so inclined to make such a statement absolute truth.

Hegel rejects the aforementioned reasoning of the dealer and the housewife and, by analogy, the reasoning behind phrenology, calling it "bad subterfuge" and he demonstrates that it lacks falsifiability because such reasoning also affirms the very opposite of what it affirms. For Hegel such lack of falsifiability is enough to run in the opposite direction of phrenology, so to speak—but when phrenology is placed in the context of a coherence epistemology perhaps a different picture emerges. This is not to say that phrenology is not a pseudoscience, but rather it is to suggest that there is a thesis (or statement being held as true) which is held as truth come what may. This thesis appears to be the one MacIntyre acknowledged—the one which can wear "phrenological clothing in 1807"

---

57. Hegel, *Phenomenology of Spirit*, 204.

and the clothing of contemporary sciences of genetics and neurophysiology today. MacIntyre never collapses this thesis into a single thesis, but instead provides the relevant thesis for phrenology[58] and then the analogous one for neurophysiology,[59] and then claims that it is a single thesis behind both. Let us say that this thesis behind both, however, is essentially that human behavior can be both generalized to a set of properties, which can be empirically observed, and in which predictions can then be made, because the set of properties is sufficient to explain the predicted behavior. It is this thesis that essentially provided an absolute statement in which a coherent web of beliefs could be structured—in 1807 this structure took the shape of phrenology—and now (according to MacIntyre) it takes the shape of genetics and neurophysiology.

MacIntyre is quite clear in his paper that the fundamental Hegelian thesis concerning how the self-consciousness should be properly understood is at odds with this aforementioned thesis. MacIntyre understands Hegel's thesis (doctrine) to have three interconnected principles. The first principle, MacIntyre explains is that "human action is characteristically neither blind and goalless nor the mere implementation of means to an already decided end ... [and that] it is only in the course of the movement that the goals of the movement are articulated is the reason why we can understand human affairs only after the event."[60] MacIntyre then reinforces this first point by making reference to Hegel's idea that the Owl of Minerva only flies at dusk. The second principle that MacIntyre understands Hegel to hold is that "Hegel did not believe that the future followed from the present simply as its rational sequel.... But it is in the working out of the failure of the present to satisfy the canons of reason that the future is made."[61] Hegel's third principle, according to MacIntyre, is that "history, informed by philosophical understanding, provides a more ultimate kind of knowledge of human beings than inquiries whose theoretical structure is modeled on that of the

---

58. Here MacIntyre explains that the relevant thesis for phrenology is that "the local activity of the brain is the sufficient cause and explanation of behavior, and that therefore the shape of the cranium allows us to predict behavior." MacIntyre, "Hegel on Faces and Skulls," 225.

59. Here MacIntyre explains the thesis to be, "that there are biochemical or neural states of affairs, processes, and events, the occurrence and the nature of which are the sufficient causes of human action." MacIntyre, "Hegel on Faces and Skulls," 225.

60. MacIntyre, "Hegel on Faces and Skulls," 234.

61. MacIntyre, "Hegel on Faces and Skulls," 234.

natural sciences."[62] These three principle are not challenged in the Hegelian system, but similarly provide an absolute in which a coherent web of beliefs can be (and, in fact, is) structured.

However, as MacIntyre rightly notes, these theses of Hegel's and the thesis which wore phrenological clothing are incompatible with each other and bring about systems of thought for comprehending the rational activity of self-consciousness which are complete opposites of each other. Verene in his chapter entitled "Phrenology" asserts that Hegel understood phrenology as being the opposite or absurd version of phenomenology, explaining that "Hegel is playing on the topsy-turvy metaphor.... Phrenology is the upside-down of phenomenology."[63] From the perspective of Hegel (or Verene's interpretation of Hegel) we can observe how Phrenology could be understood to be the inverted version of phenomenology because Hegel finds his approach to be the correct version (or right side up) and phrenology having a complete opposite thesis would result in the completely opposite claims and approach. We have also explored the idea that it is through adherence to these theses (absolute adherence) within the context of a coherence epistemology that these opposing systems remain internally coherent to those who subscribe to them, even though these system may not possess any correspondence to actuality. In the remaining section of this chapter we explore the possible reasons as to why such absolute adherence may be held to particular theses and how this practice would make the degree to which a coherence epistemology corresponded to actuality unclear.

Second Skeptical Worry: Coherence Epistemologies Make Uncertain the Degree to Which Actuality Is Experienced

When attempting to describe what Hegel's overall theory of truth is, Robert Solomon, utilizes the notion of "Self-Satisfaction." In his article entitled, "Truth and Self-Satisfaction," Solomon explains that Hegel's critique of Kantian epistemology in the third section of the *Phenomenology*, i.e., "Force and Understanding," (in which Hegel employs the topsy-turvy world thought experiment, which according to Solomon is an argument by ridicule against Kant) is equally a critique against coherent epistemologies. Solomon states that "Hegel offers us the absurd counter-example of

62. MacIntyre, "Hegel on Faces and Skulls," 235.
63. Verene, *Hegel's Recollection*, 90–91.

a "*Verkehrte*" or "inverted" world, in which black is white, light is heavy, good is evil, and so on. His ultimate target is Kant's distinction between noumenon and phenomenon, but the example holds as well against coherence theory. It is a material equivalence of the replacement of each true proposition with its contradictory, and the result is absurd."[64] Solomon finds that coherence theory is just as subject to the topsy-turvy world critique as Kant's epistemology is, because it lacks correspondence to truth as a criteria for truth, and merely argues that truth is understood as coherence within the system or within the web of beliefs. Again, this may appear to be a criticism of coherence epistemologies that begs the very question of the warranted nature of their truth claims, in that it criticizes coherence epistemologies because their truth claims lack verification of correspondence. However, it is not the lack of correspondence that we aim to emphasize, but rather the possibility of a lack of universality or consensus that one can imagine occurring from a lack of correspondence to actuality. This is essentially the content of the first skeptical discovery, which we suggest that neither Kant, nor perhaps Hegel, realized. This skeptical discovery suggests that a contingent universality or consensus among all the members of a coherent epistemology (here perhaps a better word for what is being described by the phrase "members of a coherent epistemology" is "members of a *Volksgeist*") is what ultimately makes such a system warranted—or rather unquestioned. The fact that a coherence epistemology may not correspond to actuality is a criticism only in the fact that in not corresponding to actuality it leaves open the possibility that the universal and the arbitrary need not contradict, as well as the possibility of various contradictory universalities existing within various coherent epistemologies. This makes coherence epistemologies vulnerable to the absurd, Solomon points out, because the inverse of all the claims in a coherent web of beliefs would be equally as coherent as the claims in a web of beliefs before they were all inverted. Speaking to this point, Solomon explains that "a frequent objection to the coherence theory is the following: any system of coherent beliefs can be turned into an equally coherent system by the systematic application of some logical operator, e.g. by turning each belief into its contradictory. That is there might be equally coherent but mutually incompatible systems of belief, and it would not seem to make sense to say that they are both equally 'true.'"[65]

64. Solomon, "True and Self-Satisfaction," 704.
65. Solomon, "True and Self-Satisfaction," 704.

We have already noted earlier that both MacIntyre and Verene observe that Hegel's system of phenomenology is incompatible with many systems including phrenology, behaviorism, and neurophysiology to name a few. Verene explained that Hegel viewed phrenology (and Verene viewed behaviorism) as the topsy-turvy version of phenomenology—but this conclusion—echoing the former claims of MacIntyre—appeared to be the case, not because both phenomenology and phrenology were placed in different (opposite coherence epistemologies) but rather because each system held opposite theses—theses we argued were held absolutely and transformed the coherence epistemology around such "absolute statements." Solomon, however, rejects the idea that Hegel exclusively held a coherence theory of truth, and explains rather that Hegel held what he describes as a "self-satisfaction" theory of truth. Solomon finds that both coherence and correspondence by themselves are not sufficient for a theory of truth, but rather, truth requires both that our ideas correspond to reality and that our belief systems which we use to represent and comprehend reality are coherent. Solomon explains his term "self-satisfaction," and its relation to truth, saying, "Ultimately, Truth is self-satisfaction, the optimal satisfaction of the categories which we have imposed upon our world."[66] This idea maintains that the truths we have which correspond to our world cannot be separated from the coherent framework in which the truth is ultimately understood. This relation between the coherent framework in which a truth is understood and the facts about the world that the truth corresponds to, according to Solomon, is where the idea of the absolute is paramount. The absolute is not the idea that once you have obtained absolute truth, then you will somehow know any particular empirical truth (the random example of a particular empirical truth provided by Solomon is "that one can deduce the number of rabbits in Australia,"[67]) rather it is the idea that you have philosophical criteria for truth which, "avoids skepticism and shows how it is that what we believe to be true can be known to be true."[68]

This is what Hegel attempts to do, according to Solomon—he attempts to provide a satisfactory form of mind (or category) for knowing truth, and he does this by presenting the reader with all the former forms of mind (Consciousness, Self-consciousness, Reason, and Spirit) pointing out the inadequacies or contradictions in such forms of mind, and then

---

66. Solomon, "True and Self-Satisfaction," 721.
67. Solomon, "True and Self-Satisfaction," 707.
68. Solomon, "True and Self-Satisfaction," 707.

satisfies[69] the reader with the form of mind which is absolute knowing. It is somewhat unclear, however, whether Hegel has merely formed a coherent epistemology around the three aforementioned theses which MacIntyre explained (MacIntyre finds that the three aforementioned theses are independent of, but related to, what he finds to be the overarching thesis of Hegel's entire doctrine. This thesis, according to MacIntyre, is that "all the sequences of history constitute a single movement toward the goal of a consciousness of the whole that is absolute spirit and that by its consciousness of the whole of history constitutes that whole into a single rational totality."[70]), or if he has instead provided the reader with absolute knowing. Hegel does explain that movements of the Spirit correspond to events and ideas in history, and this correspondence is made understandable in the coherent framework that he provides. It is, however, again somewhat unclear whether Hegel's system of reasoning is satisfying—and to what extent an individual might be equally satisfied with the inverse of Hegel's form of reasoning (or to what extent individuals were satisfied with forms of knowing which Hegel demonstrated to be unsatisfactory). This is to question whether such inverted form of reasoning could have been phrenology in 1807 or can still be many of our contemporary sciences currently. Is such self-satisfaction merely dependent on the customs and habits of the time which informed one of the reasonability of an underlying thesis? A further factor—one that makes this uncertainty even more complicated is whether this "Self"—or "categories which we impose on the world" is something that Hegel is attempting to create or if it is something that he has discovered by cataloging and ordering the movements of Spirit. Does Hegel satisfy the categories which his readers impose on the world, or does he persuade the reader that certain categories (a certain mind) should be the way in which we apprehend knowledge, and then provides the reader with a phenomenology which satisfies the categories that Hegel, himself

69. When explaining how the notion of Self-Satisfaction relates to truth, Solomon writes, "A *satisfactory* theory of truth, we can now say, is one which satisfies all the demands which we place on it. But this is not yet enlightening. What demands do we place upon a theory of truth? It is a mistake to think that we begin with a problem of truth, to which the various theories of truth are attempted solutions. There is no problem of truth, there are only theories of truth, whose inadequacy causes problems.... Thus the problem of truth is a problem of resolving the inadequacies created by the various theories of truth, and there we have our criterion of completeness: a satisfactory philosophical theory of truth is one which resolves all of the inadequacies of the other theories without adding new inadequacies of its own." Solomon, "True and Self-Satisfaction," 718–19.

70. MacIntyre, "Hegel on Faces and Skulls," 235.

as rendered? This question becomes our third skeptical worry which we explore in the next chapter, i.e., if we believe that it is epistemologically possible to share the mind of Spirit through comprehending the totality of Spirit's work through history, then how do we know that Hegel is sharing with us the mind of Spirit, and not merely his own point of view?

3

The Potentiality of Both the Divine Mind and the Arbitrary Particular (Human) Mind to Become Universalized

Spirit, Religion, and the Movement toward Absolute Knowing

HEGEL BEGINS HIS FIRST section on Spirit, which he entitles, "The true Spirit. The ethical order"; he further divides this section into three subsections: "The ethical world. Human and Divine Law. Man and Woman," "Ethical action. Human and Divine Knowledge. Guilt and Destiny," and "Legal status." According to Hegel, Spirit is "the substance and universal, self-identical and abiding essence, is the unmoved solid ground and starting point for the action of all, and it is their purpose and goal, the in-itself of every self-consciousness expressed in thought."[1] Spirit is more often referred to in the singular by Hegel, but he also refers to it in the plural, i.e., as "Spirits," to signify when Spirit divides itself into different moments—into various forms of substance and consciousness. Spirit divides itself, according to Hegel, so that it may provide at first a contradiction, and then so that it may further provide a resolution to the contradiction. Hegel explains that Spirit does this so that consciousness may grasp Spirit through comprehending its movements. One such division occurs, according to Hegel, in the section known as "The true Spirit. The ethical order"; this occurs when Spirit splits itself into human and divine law.

In the first two sections of this chapter, whose titles are, "The ethical world. Human and Divine Law. Man and Woman," and "Ethical action. Human and Divine Knowledge. Guilt and Destiny," Hegel presents

1. Hegel, *Phenomenology of Spirit*, 246.

his understanding of how the Spirit actualizes itself in the form of the Nation and in the form of a Family. Hegel illustrates this movement of the Spirit primarily through his commentary on Sophocles' *Antigone*. In this play, Hegel proposes that one can observe the ethical tension between the individual and the universal. The individuality finding its actualization in the family and the universal finding its actualization in the state or community. Hegel explains that in the milieu of the play, it is the role of woman to enforce the laws of the family or the Divine law (which he sometimes refers to as Penates) and it is the role of the man to enforce the laws of the community, or the human law. Spirit divides and actualizes its ethical substance into both man and woman so that each finds their respective ethical propensities to be both natural and complete. But as Hegel observes, both realize that their ethical natures are incomplete and contradictory when they come into conflict with each other. Such conflict is exemplified in the conflict between Antigone and Creon, according to Hegel, over whether it is ethical for Antigone to bury her brother.

In this ancient Greek milieu, which is provided to us by Sophocles, there exists a tension between the ethical life of the family and the ethical life of the community. This, according to Hegel, is also the tension which is present between the individuality expressed in the individual family members and the universality which is manifested in the community. The form of the Spirit which serves to resolve this tension (or rather perhaps to sublate it) according to Hegel is war, which acknowledges the worth of the individual as an individual—and each individual is able to go to war in unison, but also to perish as individuals and as a universal community (or as Hegel puts it: "and perish as individuals and as a universal, whose simple universality is soulless and dead."[2] Hegel explains that this type of individuality and universality found in this ancient Greek milieu, is overcome by a new actualization of ethical law and expression of individuality and universality, and this, according to Hegel is to be found in the milieu of ancient Rome, which is explored in the third subsection entitled, "Legal status."

In this subsection, Hegel examines the milieu of ancient Rome, and explains that the legal status of the citizen is an individuality that is based on the abstract idea that each citizen is equal. Although this status is actualized in the property laws of Rome, Hegel finds this development of the ethical order to resemble stoicism because this entire notion of individuality—although actualized—is based off an abstract idea. It is based off of

2. Hegel, *Phenomenology of Spirit*, 289.

the abstract idea of what law and, by implication, what ethical behavior should entail, as opposed to being concretized in what is perceived by a culture to be natural roles—such as in the former case of Sophocles' *Antigone*. The main difference between these two scenarios is the contingent understanding of "Legal Status" which is based solely off the ideas of the citizens. The universality is also presented in this milieu in the position of the emperor, who is a mere person, just like every other Roman citizen, and yet holds absolute authority over the community. Hegel refers to the self-consciousness of the emperor as the "titanic self-consciousness that thinks of itself as being an actual living god."[3] It is this titanic self-consciousness, which the individual self-consciousnesses of the ancient Roman milieu find themselves alienated from.[4] This is because the individuality of the citizen can naturally become at odds with the will of the emperor. This actualized alienation, Hegel finds, recapitulates the stage of self-consciousness known as the unhappy consciousness, in which one also finds such alienation. It is with this alienated self that Hegel begins the next section entitled, "Self-alienated Spirit, Culture."

After Spirit withdraws from Culture and its actuality, and inhabits instead Pure consciousness, as a way of escaping the actuality which is artificial, and which is being experienced through Culture—it inhabits Pure consciousness in two forms. These forms are "Faith" and "Pure Insight," and they are explored by Hegel in the section bearing the same name. Although Hegel utilizes the general titles of "Faith" and "Pure Insight," many commentators have suggested that Hegel is referring to the particular historical movements of Pietism on the one hand, and the Enlightenment, and perhaps the Medieval church on the other. Concerning the reference to these two movements as being historical, Lauer writes, "What we are looking at, then, are two movements in France quite clearly traceable to the bankruptcy of French culture: Pietism (with both clerical and anti-clerical repercussions), which runs right through the nineteenth century, and Enlightenment, which culminates in the French Revolution and peters out in the materialism and atheism of nineteenth and twentieth century France."[5] Hegel observes these two forms of Spirit as initially in

---

3. Hegel, *Phenomenology of Spirit*, 293.

4. On this matter Hegel writes, "Legal personality thus learns rather that it is without any substance, since the alien content makes itself authoritative in it, and does so because that content is the reality of such personality." Hegel, *Phenomenology of Spirit*, 293.

5. Lauer, *A Reading of Hegel's "Phenomenology of Spirit,"* 229.

conflict with each other; Faith possesses particular positive content for what it believes in, but it has not proceeded through a dialectical movement which would provide justification for the content believed. Pure Insight, which also withdraws from the actuality of culture, takes a negative view in response to the content of faith while providing no content of its own. This negative view of Pure Insight is expressed more thoroughly by Hegel in his next section which he titles "The Enlightenment"; this section contains two subsections which are "The struggle of the Enlightenment with Superstition," and "The truth of Enlightenment."

In the first subsection, Hegel details Pure Insight's critique of the contents of faith via the Enlightenment; while at the same time explaining that the Enlightenment aims to establish truth by reason, and attempts to legitimize such reason through this reason being accepted universally. For Hegel's readers, we find that the movement of Spirit must proceed through Faith, as opposed to Enlightenment, because Enlightenment possesses no content for Spirit to dialectically work through and establish. Faith, however, learns from the critique of the Enlightenment—it learns that it must objectify its content and make it universal by dialectically grounding it in the infinite. This, Hegel explains, faith can do in the context of religion, saying "Religion—for it is obviously religion that we are speaking about—in the form in which it appears here as the faith belonging to the world of culture, does not yet appear as it is in and for itself."[6] Hegel then provides a more detailed analysis concerning the type of truth, or way of knowing which Enlightenment provides in the subsection, "The truth of Enlightenment."

In "The truth of Enlightenment," Hegel explains that the epistemology of Enlightenment has not moved past the stages of sense certainty and perception. Enlightenment recapitulates the dialectic of sense certainty and perception so to speak, but the emphasis, for Hegel, is that the Enlightenment does not seem to fully grasp the epistemological incompleteness of its position—which is the same epistemological incompleteness found, according to Hegel, in sense certainty and perception. Enlightenment, being in this position, believes that all things consist of either pure matter or pure thought. Concerning this, Hegel states, "In this connection, it is important to bear in mind that *pure matter* is merely what is *left over* when we *abstract* from seeing, feeling, tasting, etc., i.e., it is not matter that is seen, tasted, felt, etc.; what is seen, felt, tasted, is not matter, but color, a stone, a salt, etc. Matter is rather a *pure abstraction*; and so what we are presented with here

6. Hegel, *Phenomenology of Spirit*, 322.

is the *pure essence of thought*, or pure thought itself as the Absolute, which contains no differences, is indeterminate and devoid of predicates."[7] Hegel also explains that these two positions within the Enlightenment can be distinguished as a belief in Nature as absolute or Spirit (i.e., God). Despite these differing positions within the Enlightenment, the truth of an object becomes neither that of its pure matter nor of its pure thought, but rather of its utility or usefulness to self-consciousness. Once this occurs, Hegel explains that "Consciousness has found its Notion in Utility," and once this discovery is observed, the reader moves to the third section in the chapter on Spirit, which is described by Hegel as "Absolute Freedom and Terror."

In this movement of Spirit, consciousness takes its new shape as absolute freedom, viewing the world and all the objects in it as expressions of usefulness for consciousness. It is in this section that Hegel makes reference to the idea of the general will (a concept associated with the ideas of Rousseau) in which this general will looks upon the world as serving as a form of utility for its will. This new shape of consciousness, which is absolute freedom, however, experiences Terror (here Hegel is making a reference to the Terror which historically occurred in France after the Revolution) when it is not the general will looking upon the world as usefulness, but rather it is the will of one individual or a group of individuals, which results in the meaningless deaths of many. Describing such meaningless deaths, Hegel states, "It is thus the coldest and meanest of all deaths, with no more significance than cutting off a head of cabbage or swallowing a mouthful of water."[8] At the same time that this universal will (i.e., universal in the sense that it appears that all must obey it or suffer the fate of death, in a similar sense that we might consider the will of the master, [initially] in the master-slave dialectic, a universal will—in that it is the will that all people [the two people existing in the situation—master and slave] carry out) is causing such terror and destruction, it also becomes concretized in the will of one individual (here Hegel may have the figure of Napoleon in mind.) Since one individual's will has become universalized as opposed to the general will or the will of each individual, this form of consciousness can move no further, and we must look for a form of consciousness that brings forth the will of each individual—and this Hegel believes is to be found in Morality.

In Hegel's final section on Spirit, entitled, "Spirit that is certain of itself. Morality." The reader is brought to an examination of morality in hopes to

---

7. Hegel, *Phenomenology of Spirit*, 351.
8. Hegel, *Phenomenology of Spirit*, 360.

find the freedom (absolute) which was found (concretized) for one individual (in the last form of Spirit) which is universal—i.e., we hope to find absolute freedom for all individuals. Hegel divides this section into three subsections: "The moral view of the world," "Dissemblance or duplicity," and "Conscience. The 'beautiful soul', evil and its forgiveness." In the first subsection, Hegel examines the Kantian moral philosophy, given its universality and its claim that the individual is free when they act out of duty (It is somewhat unclear whether Hegel finds any credence in this notion of freedom, i.e., when the will wills an action out of duty. What appears to be Hegel's emphasis is addressing this form of consciousness phenomenologically and pointing out features of it he deems incomplete.)—and this motivation Hegel contrast with doing something for the sake of happiness. The moral consciousness, therefore, is the consciousness that does everything out of duty and not out of happiness—and Hegel explains that happiness cannot be expected from the actions, but "only as a gift of Grace."[9] Hegel, however, points out that this moral consciousness, in actuality, cannot always will and do every moral action out of duty's sake—and when this consciousness acts, the action is actually that of another consciousness. Hegel further describes this situation by articulating two propositions. Hegel first articulates the two propositions in the following way, "'There is no *moral, perfect, actual* self-consciousness'; and since the moral sphere is at all, only in so far as it is perfect, for duty is the *pure* unadulterated *intrinsic being* or in-itself, and morality consists only in conformity to this pure in-itself—the second proposition simply runs: 'There is no moral existence in reality.'"[10] Furthermore, Hegel makes a point of restating the first proposition in relation to its existence in the imagination only, explaining that "there *is* one [here one refers to a moral, perfect, actual self-consciousness] but only in the imagination; or in other words, it is true that there is none, yet, all the same it is allowed by another consciousness to pass for one."[11]

Hegel continues to describe the unsatisfactory results of this situation as "Dissemblance or duplicity," which is the title of the following subsection. Commenting on such aforementioned dissemblance or duplicity, Lauer explains, "As Hegel sees it, Kantian morality needs a nature which is recalcitrant to it and yet wants nature to be in harmony with it."[12] This

---

9. Hegel, *Phenomenology of Spirit*, 371.
10. Hegel, *Phenomenology of Spirit*, 373.
11. Hegel, *Phenomenology of Spirit*, 374.
12. Lauer, *A Reading of Hegel's "Phenomenology of Spirit,"* 247.

situation suggests, for Hegel, that Kantian morality cannot be actualized in an authentic manner, because moral action is not the goal of Kantian morality—only having a good will is—and moral action can in no way be evaluated by the society it is actualized in because it is not possible for society to determine if an action is performed for duty's sake. This further leads Hegel to claim that the moral consciousness is not the true moral consciousness (hence the duplicity) because such morality cannot be actualized. The actual moral consciousness, for Hegel exists not in the Kantian form but elsewhere, in what he refers to as a being that "is a holy moral lawgiver." With this final insight Hegel moves to the final subsection "Conscience. The 'beautiful soul', and its forgiveness."

In this remaining subsection, Hegel first explores the form of consciousness referred to as "Conscience." This form is ostensibly an improvement from the moral consciousness which relied upon the Kantian notion of duty; Hegel finds the improvement to be that conscience does not rely upon an abstract notion of duty concerning all actions, but rather that conscience experiences an immediate conviction concerning what is right or wrong with respect to any particular action. The moral correctness for an action is therefore found in the conviction of the individual, concerning whether their action is morally right or wrong. Hegel, however, explains that the inadequacy of this position (or form of consciousness rather) is that any action can be understood as right or wrong given that it is expressed to the society by the individual, that said individual possesses the immediate conviction that the particular action is either right or wrong.

From this notion of the immediate conviction of conscience emerges what Hegel refers to as "the beautiful soul." This "beautiful soul," possesses the same immediate convictions concerning its actions as conscience; however, it refrains from action for it fears judgment from others—i.e., it fears that its actions, which it knows to be good, will be judged by others to be evil. Hegel explains that the fate of this "beautiful soul" is a "transparent purity," which results from its inaction, and because of its inaction, "its light dies within it, and it vanishes like a shapeless vapour that dissolves into thin air [para. 658]."[13] Hegel then attempts to reconcile these various forms of consciousness, i.e., the moral consciousness (which promotes the universal of duty through particular action) with the beautiful soul (which "exempts itself from the universal"—this also takes the form of the conscience which acts with conviction). The former, Hegel explains, sees the latter as evil and

---

13. Hegel, *Phenomenology of Spirit*, 400.

the latter sees the former as hypocrisy. Concerning this situation, Hegel notes, "For the consciousness which holds firmly to duty, the first consciousness counts as *evil*, because of the disparity between its *inner being* and the universal; and since, at the same time, this first consciousness declares its action to be in conformity with itself, to be duty and conscientiousness, it is held by the universal consciousness to be *hypocrisy*."[14]

The beautiful soul, though it possesses conviction, will not act; whereas the universal consciousness (which is understood to be the sum total of the convictions of others) does act and passes judgement—judgement which the beautiful soul fears. The universal moral consciousness in this situation becomes a judging consciousness and accuses the conscience of the beautiful soul of being evil—but since it judges this consciousness both negatively and arbitrarily—it shows itself to be hypocritical—and it confesses as much to the other consciousness. The consciousness which was accused of being wicked, does not reciprocate and likewise admit its own wickedness the way the former consciousness has done. However, when this mutual recognition is met—Hegel explains that Absolute Spirit, is at this point, achieved—through the confession and forgiveness between the two forms of consciousness, which were formerly at odds with each other. It is with this last development that Hegel moves toward the phenomenon of religion.

Hegel's Analysis of Religion as the Movement of Spirit

Hegel's analysis of religion as the movement of Spirit, holds that in religion, self-consciousness does not have the shape of Spirit in itself, or rather it is distinct from Spirit, and therefore, "its reality proper falls outside of religion."[15] The goal of Spirit in the milieu of Religion, as Hegel describes, becomes the "perfection of religion," which involves Spirit and self-consciousness "becoming identical with each other: not only that religion concerns itself with Spirit's reality, but conversely, that Spirit, as self-conscious Spirit, becomes actual to itself and object of its consciousness."[16] Since this is the task of religion, Hegel explains that the various forms of religion should contain the various forms of Spirit as it is striving toward the aforementioned goal—and if, therefore, the reader observes these moments of Spirit within religion,

---

14. Hegel, *Phenomenology of Spirit*, 401.
15. Hegel, *Phenomenology of Spirit*, 412.
16. Hegel, *Phenomenology of Spirit*, 412.

the totality of Spirit will be revealed. The three forms Hegel describes religion taking for this task are, "Natural Religion," "Religion as a form of Art," and "The revealed religion." Hegel states that in Natural Religion, Spirit is in the form of consciousness, whereas in Religion in the form of Art, Spirit is in the form of self-consciousness. It is only in "the revealed religion," that the Spirit experiences a unity of itself, which is a unity of consciousness and self-consciousness—i.e., Spirit being in-itself and for-itself, which according to Hegel, is Spirit's true shape.

Hegel begins with an examination of "Natural Religion," which he describes in three sections: "God as light," "Plant and animal," and "the artificer." In Natural Religion, Hegel finds Spirit present as collective consciousness in three unique ways, in three various forms of religion. The three forms of consciousness are those formerly mentioned—i.e., sense certainty, perception, and the understanding. The three religious phenomena in which the aforementioned forms of consciousness are manifested are "God as light" (which according to Hegel is manifested in the religion of Zoroastrianism); "Plant and animal" (which according to Hegel is manifested in the religions of India); and "The artificer" (which according to Hegel is manifested in the architectural projects of the Ancient Egyptian religion). The Spirit progresses through each one of these forms of religion and then moves to a form of self-consciousness as the religious activity moves from that of artificer to that of artist, in the following section, "Religion in the form of Art." Hegel finds that the association of God with light in the religion of Zoroastrianism is a manifestation of sense certainty, because it is immediate and indeterminate; it is "all-embracing," and "all pervading" as well as "formless substantiality." Much like sense certainty, light is experienced without mediation. Hegel finds the association of plants and animals with God as a manifestation of perception because, much like the objects which plants and animals are, they have particular qualities and determinations—they are essentially a thing with properties. These properties are imposed on the divine—whether such properties are peaceful such as in the case of plant life, or hostile such as in the case of some forms of animal life. Lastly, Hegel finds the association of "The artificer," and the objects such as the pyramids and obelisks with God as a manifestation of the understanding because such an object corresponds both to the phenomenal world and to the structure of our mind, i.e., consciousness of the understanding, which then moves Hegel's focus to self-consciousness.

In "Religion in the form of Art," Hegel's focuses on the Greek religion, which phenomenologically dovetails into the trust the Greeks placed in custom as well as the ethical sphere of Greek Sittlichkeit. Hegel begins with "The abstract work of Art," in which the artist creates elaborate structures and statues of the gods and of the divine realm. In this stage individuals in society interact with the gods and the divine realm, and Hegel explains that through positive interactions with the divine realm, "they receive from the grateful god a return for their gifts and proofs of his favour in which through their work they became united with him, not as a hope and in a future realization, but rather, in witnessing to his glory and in bringing him gifts, that nation has the immediate enjoyment of its own wealth and adornment."[17] In the following section, "The living work of art," Hegel highlights the transition from human beings creating statues and temples of gods, and deriving enjoyment from their interactions with them, to the divine inhabiting a particular individual within the cult of devotees. Here Hegel explains that "Man thus puts himself in the place of the statue as the shape that has been raised and fashioned for perfectly free *movement*, just as the statue is perfectly free *repose*."[18] These types of manifestations of self-consciousness by Spirit, according to Hegel, are manifested both in "Bacchic enthusiasm," and in the ancient Greek athletic games. The latter manifests spiritual essence in "corporeal beauty," and the former merely being "beside itself."

Hegel then proceeds to the final stage of Religion as a form of Art in Greek culture—this stage is poetry. Hegel notes the three types of poetry in which the Greek gods are experienced by society; these types being epic, tragedy, and comedy. Hegel explains that it is only through the latter that the self-consciousness becomes aware of both itself, and that it—i.e., the community—as artist is the creator of these gods. Here Hegel writes that "the self, appearing here in its significance as something actual, plays with the mask which it once put on in order to act its part; but it as quickly breaks out again from this illusory character and stands forth in its own nakedness and ordinariness, which it shows to be not distinct from the genuine self, the actor, or from the spectator."[19] Once the self-consciousness is aware that it is the creator of such gods, it is then free to contemplate the character of the divine utilizing rational thought as opposed to drawing from the contingent

17. Hegel, *Phenomenology of Spirit*, 435.
18. Hegel, *Phenomenology of Spirit*, 438.
19. Hegel, *Phenomenology of Spirit*, 450.

forms of the gods expressed in art. It is at this point that Hegel introduces the stage of "The revealed religion," but before proceeding to "The revealed religion," he elaborates more on the former stage, explaining that "This self-certainty is a state of spiritual well-being and of repose therein, such as is not to be found anywhere outside of this Comedy."[20] Although it is in this comic consciousness that Hegel finds the demise of the belief in ancient Greek divinities occurs—it is ultimately in the unhappy consciousness where the full effect of such a demise is comprehended.

In "The revealed religion," Hegel draws upon the Christian doctrine of the incarnation as a way of uniting Spirit as consciousness observed in Natural Religion and Spirit as self-consciousness, observed in "Religion as a form of Art." In the person of Jesus Christ we are shown a consciousness that is both fully human and fully divine. Concerning this Hegel writes, "The divine nature is the same as the human, and it is this unity that is beheld."[21] This form of consciousness is revealed in the incarnation, but it is not universalized until the resurrection in which a universal self-consciousness, which is Spirit (Here "Spirit" in the Hegelian sense of the term appears to conflate itself with the Christian notion of the Holy Spirit), inhabits the self-consciousness of the religious community. With this movement of Spirit complete, Spirit now exists in-itself and for-itself, in the self-consciousness of the religious community. The only thing remaining for the self-consciousness of the religious community to achieve is to completely identify with this form of self-consciousness, which was revealed in the incarnation and universalized in the resurrection. This complete identification is understood by Hegel as "Absolute Knowing,"—the final "movement" of the Spirit.

How Absolute Knowing Is Explained to Provide Truth

After providing the reader with various forms of consciousness, self-consciousness, Reason, and Spirit, which culminated in the community Spirit of the revealed religion—Hegel explains that there is one more step remaining for the reader to take (which is also to say that there is one more step left for Spirit itself to take through the mutual actions of the reader). This step is absolute knowing. In this last chapter of the *Phenomenology*, Hegel provides the reader with a summary of the various stages of Spirit. The task

20. Hegel, *Phenomenology of Spirit*, 453.
21. Hegel, *Phenomenology of Spirit*, 460.

of presenting the movements of Spirit which was originally presented in the former chapters leading up to absolute knowing, is described by Hegel as, "our *own* act here has been simply to *gather together* the separate moments, each of which in principle exhibits the life of Spirit in its entirety, and also to stick to the Notion in the form of the Notion, the content of which would already have yielded itself in those moments and in the form of a *shape of consciousness.*"[22] In this last chapter, Hegel aims to have the reader comprehend how all former forms of consciousness have led up to the form of shared consciousness, portrayed in the community corresponding to revealed religion. Hegel aims to have the reader comprehend that this form of consciousness is necessarily the Notion—i.e., that this consciousness is both human consciousness and divine consciousness. With this last chapter, Hegel aims to have the reader comprehend that this form of consciousness is their natural form of consciousness, i.e., that their essence and the essence of the Notion are the same. This absolute knowing is grounded in the larger context of absolute idealism, which as Willem deVries correctly explains "is principally a metaphysical position characterizable as the claim that mind and reality share the same categorical structure."[23] Fully comprehending this structure shared by mind (both human and divine) and reality, and realizing that this particular structure of mind is ones natural structure is understood, by Hegel, as Absolute Knowing.

This latter aim which Hegel hopes to accomplish in the chapter on absolute knowing is of particular importance because it is what will provide certainty to the reader. It will provide a certainty that their form of self-consciousness is in no way inadequate—nor does their self-consciousness possess any of the shortcomings which the prior forms of consciousness had. Hegel finds that if such certainty is established, the reader will realize that "this last shape of Spirit—the Spirit which at the same time gives its complete and true content the form of the self and thereby realizes its Notion as remaining in its Notion in this realization—this is absolute knowing."[24] One can be certain that they have truth concerning the nature of an object, because—if one is convinced by Hegel's argument—Hegel has shown that the subject and the object are categorically the same, each having their identity in the Notion. Absolute knowing ultimately rest on whether one finds Hegel's account of the various forms of Spirit convincing, as a portrayal

---

22. Hegel, *Phenomenology of Spirit*, 485.
23. deVires, "Hegel's Logic and Philosophy of Mind," 218.
24. Hegel, *Phenomenology of Spirit*, 485.

of the necessary unfolding of the work of Spirit throughout history, which results in the unity of the human and the divine mind in the religious community.[25] And then after such a presentation of this history of Spirit has occurred one must then find its phenomenological presentation by Hegel to be an accurate portrayal of one's own self-consciousness.

In the following sections we will examine our third skeptical discovery in relation to absolute knowing. Particularly, we will examine the concern that what Hegel has presented to us may not be an objective, necessary unfolding of Spirit throughout history, but rather that it is merely a product of Hegel's own creativity—which is not to say that it is not a fascinating form of self-consciousness and even has the possibility of becoming universalized. We, however, will question whether—even if such universality of this form of self-consciousness were to take place—this chapter on absolute knowing is an actual presentation of the divine mind or whether it is merely a description of the mind of Hegel. We will examine this third skeptical discovery first through an examination of Voegelin's thesis which accuses Hegel of Sorcery when he presents the *Phenomenology* as a path which leads to absolute knowing. Second, we will examine this third skeptical discovery through a development of Voegelin's thesis based on the many forms of dominating, duplicating, and universalized consciousnesses presented throughout the *Phenomenology*.

An Examination of Voegelin's Thesis

"On Hegel—A Study in Sorcery" by Eric Voegelin has rightly been referred to as a "savagely polemical essay," in which "Voegelin never adequately developed his thesis."[26] In this article Voegelin makes a few distinct but interrelated claims about what he suspects Hegel is doing when rendering the *Phenomenology of Spirit*. The first distinct claim is that Hegel is providing his audience with "imaginative history" when he shares the phenomenological movements of Spirit. When describing what imaginative history precisely is, Voegelin explains that "Hegel's choice of an imaginary absolute pole was "Empire," understood as the ecumenic organization of mankind

---

25. Here I find that one could make a very convincing argument that Hegel is unsuccessful in demonstrating this necessary unfolding of the work of the Spirit throughout history—however, I find that one would have a much more difficult time attempting to provide a convincing argument that Hegel is not, in fact, attempting to demonstrate this.

26. Magee, *Hegel and the Hermetic Tradition*, 6.

under the Idea in history; and the deformation of the cognitive core imposed the deformed style of cognition which produced the imaginary history of the Idea."[27] Voegelin then describes the *Phenomenology* in the context of this "imaginary history," by explaining that "the *Phaenomenology* has 564 pages; and it ranges with an incredible wealth of observations over such phenomena as the relation of master and servant; Stoicism, Scepticism, and the unhappy consciousness; existentialist attitudes such as the hedonist and the moralist; apolitical and political man, revolutionary and loyal citizen; classical tragedy and Christian religion; alienation, education, faith, intellectualism; enlightenment, superstition, freedom, and terror; the French Revolution and the Napoleonic Empire. In Hegel's construction, all of these phenomena are meant to be stages in the dialectical process of immanent consciousness toward its goal of 'absolute knowledge.'"[28] After describing this imaginative history—which Voegelin considers as neither an accurate portrayal of the empirical past nor a valid account of the necessary movements of the Spirit—Voegelin presents his second distinct point, that Hegel has created a grimoire, when he rendered the *Phenomenology of Spirit*, and that this grimoire is not a harmless product of the imagination, but rather something with greater destructive power.

Concerning this grimoire and its destructive capacity Voegelin writes,

> but the reader, living in his common sense habits, will understand the frequently brilliant observations as a philosopher's [Hegel's] reflections on phenomena in the real world of personal existence in society and history. The *Phaenomenology* is a divertissement in the pregnant sense of an imaginative game, masterly devised so close to reality that the excited spectator may forget that what he is watching is no more than a game.... The structure of the game must be isolated and recognized, but it must not be torn out of the context of the grimoire. Hegel does not want to play games for their sake, he wants to find the *Zauberworte* that will give him power over reality. And in its context, the game is not the diverting escape from reality as which it appears to the critical reader, but the necessary means for the end of establishing the "real knowledge" that will enable Hegel to evoke the shape of the future.[29]

Much of Voegelin's thesis, however, has not been elucidated because Voegelin does not simply accuse Hegel of making a grimoire and

27. Voegelin, "On Hegel," 437.
28. Voegelin, "On Hegel," 426.
29. Voegelin, "On Hegel," 426–27.

of practicing sorcery; Voegelin also believes that by making the grimoire, Hegel has violently destroyed reality. Voegelin believes that Hegel has destroyed reality in the sense that he has distorted the past in such a way that the future that would have followed from the past will now no longer follow. Inasmuch Voegelin states, "The construction of a grimoire is a violent destruction of reality."[30] How might we ask, is the construction of the *Phenomenology of Spirit* a violent destruction of reality?

The fact that this question is never answered by Voegelin, demonstrates the cogency of McGee's assertion that Voegelin never fully developed his thesis—but let us now explore the idea that the thesis can quite easily be developed by considering the first skeptical discovery, which is that what is universal and what is arbitrary need never contradict. Voegelin's accusations suggest that Hegel is taking the reality of both the historical knowledge and religious knowledge, which make up the self-consciousness of his readership, and he is replacing this self-consciousness, with the arbitrary self-consciousness Hegel has produced through his telling of imaginative history. If Hegel's readership finds his summary of the movement of the Spirit convincing, which the final chapter of the *Phenomenology*, entitled "Absolute Knowing," seeks to do with a summary of the activity of Spirit, then the reader will experience a certainty that the structure of their self-consciousness is naturally the same as the structure of the self-consciousness which Hegel has described in the *Phenomenology*. Voegelin's thesis appears to suggest that what sorcery amounts to in this situation is the strategy that Hegel is using to convince people (i.e., having people read the "grimoire" which Voegelin understands the *Phenomenology* to be, and from their reading they become convinced that its contents are true) that a self-consciousness, which is entirely Hegel's own creation, is both their natural mind and the mind of God. Even if his self-consciousness became universal, according to Voegelin's thesis, it would still be arbitrary and it would bring Hegel's readership no closer to the truth, because it is merely a product of Hegel's own mind.

Voegelin appears again to suggest that the success Hegel has in convincing individuals that he has accurately presented the path of Spirit for the purpose of absolute knowing rests in the strategy Hegel employees of having his imaginative history closely resemble actually history at certain points, while making insightful comments and summaries of such points in history. This activity of Hegel, Voegelin describes as "the construction

---

30. Voegelin, "On Hegel," 427.

of a grimoire," and he claims that in its construction there is "a violent destruction of reality," because Voegelin finds that Hegel has not presented his readers with an accurate representation of the activities of Spirit[31]—and in doing so has also not presented the readers with the divine mind. Rather, Voegelin accuses Hegel of manipulating his readers into thinking that his mind is the divine mind to "enable Hegel to evoke the shape of the future" and to "give him power of reality." It is not our aim in this manuscript to argue for or against Voegelin's thesis, but rather to address the third skeptical discovery which arises as a result of this thesis. We inquire as to how we know that Hegel is not (intentionally as Voegelin suggests, or unintentionally which seems more reasonable to initially argue) providing his audience with a description of a self-consciousness which is merely a creation of his own mind and not the divine mind, which is perceived from the totality of the activity of Spirit. It is the position of this manuscript that we are unable to epistemologically discern which of the former two options the case, in fact, is. Ironically the *Phenomenology*, although it argues quite elaborately that the activity of the divine mind has been presented, also portrays a variety of what we might call "dominating consciousness" while it presents the activity of Spirit. The most salient example of a dominating consciousness occurs in "The law of the heart and the frenzy of self-conceit." We will explore this and other forms of dominating consciousnesses in the remaining section—but these dominating consciousnesses present a very interesting epistemological option concerning the compatibility of the arbitrary and the universal. In these situations we have an individual self-consciousness in which aspects of this individual self-consciousness are universalized within the particular milieu. Such universalization is contingent and the particular individual is arbitrary. Voegelin's thesis essentially asserts that Hegel is just another such individual, who understood that an individual's self-consciousness has the possibility to be universalized and he designed a grimoire (the *Phenomenology*) in an attempt to make this possibility an actuality. In the following section, we will examine how this possibility obscures epistemological certainty concerning whether Hegel has actually presented the activity of Spirit, and with it the divine mind, or if Hegel has merely presented a self-consciousness of his own creation.

---

31. One should note that it remains unclear whether Voegelin does in fact believe there even is a movement of Spirit—but it is evident that he does not believe Hegel has access to an apprehension of Spirit.

THE DIVINE MIND AND THE ARBITRARY PARTICULAR MIND

Developing Voegelin's Thesis through an Examination of "The Law of the Heart and the Frenzy of Self-Conceit," and Other Forms of Dominating Consciousness

Before we continue to examine the third skeptical discovery, the discovery that if we believe it is epistemologically possible to share the mind of Spirit through comprehending the totality of Spirit's works through history, then how do we know that Hegel is sharing with us the mind of Spirit, and not merely his own point of view? It may be helpful when examining this third skeptical discovery to review and further examine examples in the *Phenomenology* where aspects of consciousness have in fact been shared, universalized, or duplicated. As we examine these various phenomena, we will ask whether it appears more likely that Hegel is simply attempting to universalize his self-consciousness. We will ask whether such examples end up adding credence to Voegelin's accusations, or whether Hegel is doing something categorically different than what he presents concerning other self-conscoiusnesses manifesting their minds in others. Let us turn to the first part of the *Phenomenology of Spirit* where Hegel discusses duplicating the individual mind such that it becomes "the form of universality."[32] This is discussed in the chapter of Reason in the section entitled "The law of the heart and the frenzy of self-conceit." Prior to this section self-consciousness has moved from observing an object, to observing itself as an object, to realizing that it should exist in and for itself. The self-consciousness moves away from observation and toward activity that manifests itself—and this activity quickly leads to an examination of ethical activity and social life. This new examination begins a shift in focus in the *Phenomenology* from epistemology to ethics and social life—with the emphasis now being on manifesting self-consciousness as it is in itself and for itself.

Prior to this transition fully taking place—a transition in which virtue is used to combat particular individualities from becoming universal—we encounter a situation in which a form of self-consciousness appears to succeed (temporarily) in universalizing itself. The stage of self-consciousness

---

32. It was considered to begin with the Master-slave dialectic because this is the first case in the *Phenomenology* where Hegel describes one mind dominating and essentially taking over the mind of another—this was also quite an elaborate account of such a process. However, the example of the Heart's law was chosen primarily because of its emphasis on universality given the larger society (milieu). That being said, the Master-slave dialect is a great example of the universalization of the Master's mind, but since there is only two individuals in this example—universalization may not be the best way of describing what occurs.

in which this appears to happen, Hegel refers to as "the law of the heart and the frenzy of self-conceit." Some commentators, such as Loewenberg, have suggested that the inspiration or prototype for such an individual as Hegel describes who makes (or attempts to make) his heart's law universal can be found in the characters of fictional writings by authors such as Goethe and Schiller. Loewenberg (through the character dialogue of "Hardith") writes, "The romantic reformer, such as Hegel portrays him strikes me as a contrived caricature. Hegel no doubt has in mind the sentimental literature of his time. Unmistakable, for example, are the allusions to Goethe's *Werther* and Schiller's *Robbers*. And it is difficult not to think of Rousseau in connection with Hegel's general attack on sentimentalism."[33] This self-consciousness, having inspirational elements that are both factual and fictional, firmly believes that in the law of their heart exists the blueprint to reform society and, therefore, this self-consciousness seeks to universalize their heart's law. Hegel makes use of the word "heart" as opposed to "mind," to emphasize the fact that from Hegel's point of view the impetus for such universalization lacks any correspondence to Reason which could be universalized. Let us explore this shape of self-consciousness as a way of examining how Hegel appears to find that arbitrary laws/desires of a particular heart can become universalized. After examining this attempt at universalization we will then compare this phenomenon to the manner in which Voegelin has described Hegel's actions of attempting to provide justification for universalizing absolute knowing.

In "The Law of the Heart and the frenzy of self-conceit," we encounter a situation in which an individual's self-consciousness has a particular and immediate awareness (a realization) of what is good and bad, right and wrong. Hegel, when introducing this section explains to the reader that "we have to see whether its realization corresponds to this Notion and whether in that realization it will find that this its law is its essential nature."[34] As the reader proceeds through this section, it becomes apparent that the "law of the heart" does not provide the essential nature (i.e., the essential nature concerning what morality is) because it is both immediate and particular. The particularity is such that if the particular heart's law were to become universalized it would not take into consideration that all other people likewise have a particular law of the heart—and if their laws were not likewise actualized, but instead only the particular

33. Loewenberg, *Hegel's Phenomenology*, 158.
34. Hegel, *Phenomenology of Spirit*, 221.

heart's law of another was actualized—then such a law would be both oppressive and arbitrary in their perspective.

The reader, however, has not learned of the impending failure of this form of self-consciousness at this point in Hegel's explanation, and so the reader proceeds to observe as this form of consciousness attempts to universalize its law of the heart. Hegel describes this moment of the heart's movement toward universalization by stating that "this heart is confronted by a real world,"[35] which is to say that the world in which this heart is operating in does not share its particular view, and is therefore opposed to the law of this heart. Given the opposition which the heart experiences in the world, the heart views the world as oppressing it. This individual works, therefore, to change the world that opposes it, and to make the world correspond to the law of its heart. It does this all the while assuming that the particular law in its heart is a law that is universally shared in all hearts—but this is not the case, and this heart has not yet realized this fact. Concerning the effort and frame of mind of this heart, Hegel writes, "What it realizes is itself the law, and its pleasure is therefore at the same time the universal pleasure of all hearts. To it the two are undivided; its pleasure is what conforms to the law, and the realization of the law of universal humanity procures for it its own particular pleasure."[36]

Then, although Hegel does not provide particular details concerning how such an achievement occurs, he explains, "The individual, then, carries out the law of his heart. This becomes a universal ordinance, and pleasure becomes a reality which absolutely conforms to law."[37] Here it appears that the individual has succeeded in changing the "authoritative divine and human ordinances," into the law of its particular heart—and it has furthermore convinced itself that it does this for the benefit of humanity. It is at this point that Hegel explains that this form of consciousness begins to break down because it has designed for itself a contradictory situation. Particularly, Hegel states, "His deed, qua actuality, belongs to the universal; but its content is his own individuality which, as this particular individuality wants to preserve itself in opposition to the universal."[38] We must wonder whether such a situation and outcome must necessarily be the case. What Hegel has shown is that a particular individual can (at least for a brief time)

35. Hegel, *Phenomenology of Spirit*, 221.
36. Hegel, *Phenomenology of Spirit*, 222.
37. Hegel, *Phenomenology of Spirit*, 223.
38. Hegel, *Phenomenology of Spirit*, 224.

universalize their will in their particular milieu (or perhaps they cannot succeed in universalizing their will but they nevertheless attempt to do just that). Hegel then proceeds to argue that such a universalization is unstable, because in its realization it manifests a contradiction. It remains, however, not thoroughly demonstrated why such a situation could not persist—or to what extent (duration), such a situation could persist. Put another way, if the individual sincerely believes that the law of its heart is the law of all hearts, and that actualizing such a law would be of great benefit to humanity, then it seems unclear why in actualizing such a law, the situation would necessarily "turn against him." It may seem that "the world" would reject such an individual, but only if they remained unconvinced by him. To further speak to this point concerning the lack of necessity in Hegel's portray of the fate of the reformer who is aiming to universalize the law of his heart, Loewenberg (through the character Hardith) explains,

> The pity he [the reformer] feels is for his own heart so deeply injured by a cruel world. And so "the heart-throb for the welfare of humanity," say Hegel, with evident allusion to Schiller's early drama, "passes into the rage of frantic self-conceit." Unaware of thus betraying his egoism and vanity, he continues to cherish his ideal for a world not deserving it. Whence necessity for such a conclusion? Hegel seems to have allowed an individual example drawn from fiction to prescribe the development of a situation alleged to be typical. Would the dialect have here taken this particular turn if it had not been modeled on a single literary product? One wonders.[39]

Loewenberg's conclusion of "one wonders" appears to be indicating that had such fictional writers as Goethe and Schiller not provided Hegel with such characters as fictional templates of the law of the heart, and a corresponding narrative to follow, then the particular conclusion which Hegel describes concerning such an individual may have been entirely different. Or the individual may have not been recognizably present in the phenomenology at all—given the fictional (as opposed to historical) nature. It is unclear however, again, given the fictional nature of the entire account, whether one could succeed in universalizing their heart's law. At this point however, if may be significant to note, that if one could, Hegel seems to have failed to present an adequate argument for why such

---

39. Loewenberg, *Hegel's Phenomenology*, 161.

universalization would necessarily fail and result in the particular outcome that he has described.

The situation further disintegrates, according to Hegel, because as the particular heart is essentially duplicated (for a time in others) as it is universalized in the laws that other citizens must obey, these other citizens reject this particularity (being universalized) in favor of their own particularity. Describing this development, Hegel states, "Consequently, others do not find in this content the fulfilment of the law of *their* hearts, but rather that of someone else; and precisely in accordance with the universal law that each shall find in what is law *his* own heart, they turn against the reality *he* set up, just as he turned against theirs."[40] This heart now reimagines the former ordinances, not as a law that is essentially at odds with and oppressing its particular heart's law, but rather as "the law of every heart"; a law that does not mirror the particularity of any one individual heart, but rather one that provides universal, generally acceptable ordinances to all citizens, favoring no particular heart. Once this individual realizes that their particular law of the heart is not essential to the law of all hearts, Hegel explains that "an insane self-conceit," arises in the individual as it attempts to "preserve itself from destruction"; a destruction it sees as certain because its particularity is inessential to the law of all hearts. However, Hegel also informs us that the law of all hearts is really "only a universal resistance and struggle of all against one another in which each claims validity for his own individuality."[41] Hegel refers to this dynamic as "the way of the world." He also describes such universality as "the essenceless play of establishing and nullifying individualities."[42]

If we examine what occurs in "The law of the Heart and the frenzy of self-conceit," a few interesting questions arise concerning Voegelin's thesis. To begin with, it can appear as though Voegelin is accusing Hegel of doing something strikingly similar to what Hegel describes this particular "heart" to be doing in "The law of the Heart and the frenzy of self-conceit." Voegelin is suggesting that Hegel is attempting to universalize his mind, by persuading his audience that a form of self-consciousness is not merely his mind, but naturally their mind as well as the divine mind. Voegelin considers such a move an attack, ultimately on reality, and expresses as much when he states, "That is the attack Hegel commits when he replaces the concrete

40. Hegel, *Phenomenology of Spirit*, 224.
41. Hegel, *Phenomenology of Spirit*, 227.
42. Hegel, *Phenomenology of Spirit*, 227.

consciousness of concrete man by the imaginary "consciousness" that runs its dialectical course in time to the absolute consciousness of Self in his System."[43] The heart also attempts to universalize its mind, and replace the current ordinances with ones that perfectly reflect its own mind—but it does not ultimately succeed. The reason given for its failure is twofold: First, this movement toward universality fails because it does not correspond with the notion—which is the one correspondence that can legitimately be universalized. Second, this law of the heart fails to sustain its universalization because, as Hegel explains, the other members of society reject the idea of a particular individual law of the heart being universalized. They realize that they are also individuals and find a particular arbitrary heart universalizing itself to be oppressive—and find more value in the former law, which is described as "the law of all hearts."

Although he never explicitly says as much, Voegelin appears to reject the idea that there is a Notion to which history is corresponding. Concerning Hegel's endeavors in the *Phenomenology*, Voegelin voices his opposition to the project's very nature by explaining, "To imagine the search for truth not to be the essence of humanity but an historical imperfection of knowledge to be overcome, in history, by perfect knowledge that will put an end to the search, is an attack on man's consciousness of his existence under God."[44] At the very least, Voegelin does not believe that Hegel has discovered the movements of Spirit in history and has understood them sufficiently to comprehend the divine mind. Again, recall that Voegelin characterizes Hegel's attempt to organize historical events, in the fashion that he does, as imaginative history. Similarly, Voegelin appears to think that individuals are also prone to being convinced—by Hegel's presentation of imaginative history—of something that is not true. What Voegelin sees as this manipulative power[45] at work in the *Phenomenology* to persuade his readers that his mind should be universally adopted is what Voegelin labels as sorcery—and this is what he accuses Hegel of.

If we return again to "The law of the Heart and the frenzy of self-conceit," and we ask again why such a law of the heart failed—or perhaps we ask the same question in a different way, namely, "How could the law

43. Voegelin, "On Hegel," 428.
44. Voegelin, "On Hegel," 428.
45. Concerning such manipulation, Voegelin referring to Hegel explains that "Only a master of philosophical technique could have devised the construction of "consciousness" just analyzed; but then again no philosopher would ever indulge in such a construction." Voegelin, "On Hegel," 429.

THE DIVINE MIND AND THE ARBITRARY PARTICULAR MIND

of a particular heart succeed in universalizing itself?" Voegelin's accusations provide an interesting answer. (An answer that perhaps adds a bit more credence to his accusations—though perhaps not making them fully compelling) This answer is that the particular heart failed to convince the other members of society that its particular heart was actually something shared by the rest of society, and should therefore naturally be universalized. This, Hegel does (or attempts to do) through intellectual persuasion, by (according to Voegelin) the telling of imaginative history, in such a way that his audience is compelled ultimately, by the claim of absolute knowing. Hegel experiences success, whereas the particular heart experiences failure because Hegel is able to provide an elaborate (and possibly manipulative account according of Voegelin) account of the movements of Spirit, such that he convinces his audience that he has observed the divine mind which should be universalized in the human community. Given the interpretative and polemical thesis that Voegelin utilizes to characterize Hegel's project of the *Phenomenology*—as well as the contrast of Hegel's chapter on absolute knowing meant to persuade the reader, with the account of the failure of the law of the heart—it is difficult to know precisely what has occurred when, or if, one finds Hegel's account of absolute knowing persuasive.

Due to this difficultly we find that agnosticism toward Hegel's conclusion of absolute knowing is tentatively appropriate and our aim will be to explore this further in the remainder of this chapter. This difficultly which we argue promotes agnosticism is exacerbated by the frequency of what we might refer to as various forms of "dominating consciousnesses" which are presented by Hegel throughout the *Phenomenology*. We ascribe the phrase "dominating consciousness" to denote any consciousness that attempts to duplicate or universalize an aspect of its mind in the mind of another self-consciousness. This duplication or universalization could be through force, persuasion, or through the very structure of a society; it could be intentional or unintentional (on the part of the individual—but, according to Hegel, it would be necessary from the perspective of Spirit). We have selected the law of the heart because this form of consciousness appeared to provide the most elaborate treatment of this phenomenon, but there are many other examples of this phenomenon of consciousness in the *Phenomenology*. For example, there is the Master or Lord that physically subdues the servant upon threat of death, and leaves the servant's mind preoccupied with the will of the Master, so much so that for a time the Master's mind is duplicated in the mind of the servant.[46] There is the priestly mediator, who provides instruction for the unhappy consciousness to obey; there is the absolute power of the emperor—what Hegel refers to as the "titanic consciousness"—over all citizens of Rome during Roman times. Again we find the absolute power of the monarch in France, in which all citizens pledge their allegiance and continually flatter this absolute consciousness with their words; and there is what is supposed to be the general will of all citizens, becoming the particular will of one individual—Hegel alludes to this individual in the concrete example of Napoleon.

Hegel has provided his readers with such a rich variety of dominating consciousnesses that one cannot help but wonder whether his project is just another such example of such a form of consciousness—albeit, a much more elaborate and sophisticated form of it. Voegelin, obviously believes this to be the case, but he simply accuses Hegel of this as opposed to making an argument justifying such accusations. In this chapter, we have developed Voegelin's thesis in an attempt to show what the compelling aspects of it are. Our position is not one of agreement with the conclusions of Voegelin, but rather, we find that he puts forth a thesis which provokes sufficient doubt when one reexamines the *Phenomenology* with this thesis in mind. It is enough doubt that when Hegel's *Phenomenology* is viewed in its entirety it remains unclear as to whether Hegel has provided an accurate account of and path toward absolute knowing—or whether it is the case, as Voegelin charges, that Hegel is merely passing off a form of self-consciousness that he created as (and is merely a product of his own mind) the divine mind. (There is also the possibility that Hegel earnestly believes he has discovered the divine mind, but that he is mistaken in his conviction.) In the next chapter we explore the implications of this third skeptical discovery in combination with the implications of the former two skeptical discoveries. We argue that these three skeptical discoveries taken in combination provide justification for an agnosticism that results in the indistinguishability between the arbitrary and non-arbitrary nature of things.

---

46. Note, this situation of the Master's mind being duplicated in the mind of the servant, only last for a brief time, before the master, so to speak, becomes the servant, and the servant, the master.

Further Considerations on the Meaning of Dominating Consciousness

The idea of a "dominating consciousness" was developed after some reflection on Voegelin's thesis. The insights drawn from Voegelin can prove difficult to disentangle for Voegelin's accusations toward Hegel's project, as well as his disagreement with Hegel's ontology. As previously mentioned, it remains unclear whether Voegelin subscribed to an ontology which would allow for the very idea of Spirit revealing itself in history. It is, however, certain that Voegelin concluded that Hegel did not have access to such knowledge. To further complicate matters Voegelin accuses Hegel of subterfuge when constructing the *Phenomenology*. Insights, which occur when examining Voegelin's ideas must therefore also be distinguished from his suspicions of Hegel.

What remains noteworthy after reading Voegelin's comments on Hegel is the frequency to which forms of consciousness which Hegel describes in the *Phenomenology* appear to exert or attempt to exert control over others. This phenomenon appears noteworthy, particularly because Voegelin accuses Hegel of attempting to do such a thing himself—of attempting to universalize his own fictions as facts in the minds of others. This type of action seems to be the essence of the "dominating consciousness"—to make their particular will universal. The form of consciousness that appears to exemplify this tendency blatantly and in the grandest way is "the Law of the Heart"—but Hegel's descriptions of the "titanic consciousness" of the Roman Empire and the "absolute consciousness" of the monarch of France appear close seconds. Removed from the ontology of Spirit, we appear to observe Hegel describing single, particular consciousnessess dominating—i.e., exerting their will over the masses. Voegelin, I suspect, envisions Hegel as attempting to do the same, only with greater cleverness and sophistication.

4

Parting Company with Hegel after an Examination of Three Skeptical Discoveries

An Examination of "Religion in the Form of Art"

IN COMMENTING ON THE results of absolute knowing, in Hegel's *Phenomenology*, Lauer, explains "One thing at least is clear: only after a second reading can we in conscience either go along with Hegel or part company with him."[1] Shortly thereafter however, Lauer further explains that "of course, the reader of the *Phenomenology* runs into a difficulty which perhaps even a second reading will not eliminate: the ways in which spirit appears are the ways it has appeared to Hegel; what guarantee is there that they are either necessary or complete? None. It is simply up to the reader to judge, having examined them carefully, whether Hegel's account is convincing."[2] In this chapter we will examine how the three aforementioned skeptical discoveries provoke enough doubt as to not find Hegel's account of absolute knowing fully convincing—and why, as Lauer explains, we must then "part company with him." The aim of this chapter, therefore, is twofold: First, it is to explain why the three skeptical discoveries, when jointly considered, provoke enough doubt to make Hegel's presentation of absolute knowing less than fully convincing. Second, we aim to explain what the result of parting company with Hegel (and with absolute knowing) is, while still retaining such doubts epistemologically. Concerning the latter aim, this chapter argues that epistemological agnosticism (concerning whether the nature of things is non-arbitrary) is the most cogent stance after parting company with Hegel, while retaining

---

1. Lauer, *A Reading of Hegel's "Phenomenology of Spirit,"* 287.
2. Lauer, *A Reading of Hegel's "Phenomenology of Spirit,"* 288.

such doubts. In this chapter, we will argue that such epistemological agnosticism is best expressed as a belief in the indistinguishability between the arbitrary and non-arbitrary nature of things.

Associating Hegel's Use of Gestalt with the Idea of Coherence Epistemology

Prior to his chapter on Religion, Hegel has shown us dimensions of Spirit, as consciousness, self-consciousness, Reason, and Spirit outside of the context of what we now call the "religions of the world." In his chapter on religion, however, he describes the progression of Spirit through the religions of the world. Each religion has its own Gestalt or shape of Spirit in which the people of that particular Spirit experience as coherent. Being of a particular Spirit, i.e., having a sustained form of religious life allows the particular people to understand the world in a particular way. However, Hegel puts forward the argument that the concept of the divine in each of these religions is incomplete and therefore has not been fully manifested in-itself and for-itself. The Spirit, therefore, moves from religions of nature, to those of art, and finally to revealed religion.

The word "Gestalt" is quite a fortuitous word to use when describing "shapes of Spirit" particularly given the phenomenon of ambiguous figures which have become emblematic of Gestalt psychology. The connection here being that an ambiguous figure can be seen in an unambiguous way (so much so that the individual may not even be aware of the ambiguity of the figure) by an individual approaching the figure with a certain frame (Gestalt) of mind. That same ambiguous figure, however, can be seen in a contrary unambiguous way by another individual approaching the figure with a different frame of mind. The shape of Spirit found in each religion Hegel explores approaches the divine in an incomplete yet unambiguous way (according to Hegel), and therefore, comprehends an unambiguous yet incomplete understanding of the divine. It is not until Hegel explains revealed religion in philosophical terms that the reader (according to Hegel) is able to comprehend the divine in unambiguous and complete terms. This final step or movement of Spirit is understood as absolute knowing.

In this section we would like to explore the idea that the reason Hegel's epistemology has often been mistakenly understood as a form of coherence epistemology is due to the fact that the German word "Gestalt" or "Gestalten," which Hegel is fond of using when describing the "form" or "shape" of Spirit could be conceptually substituted with the word "coherence" with respect to how the term "coherence" is understood in reference to the concept of coherence epistemology. This conceptual substitution of the word "coherence" for the word "Gestalt" would only be appropriate in the context of the reader's exploration of the various forms of consciousness which Hegel provides, and it would not be an appropriate substitution of the individual self-consciousness enveloped in the milieu of the particular form of consciousness which Hegel is describing. For the latter individual, the epistemology experienced would be best characterized as that of correspondence (from the individual's perspective)—having the same certainty for the individual as sense certainty initially appears to have at the outset of the *Phenomenology*. So, for example, the reader of Hegel's *Phenomenology*, when reading about ancient Greek society, experiences this particular form of Spirit or consciousness as one form among many. The reader experiences this form as a form of consciousness not necessarily corresponding to anything actual in the reality they are immersed in, but rather still experiences how this form of consciousness coheres with itself. The reader can then imagine how this form of consciousness may appear to provide certainty for individuals in that particular milieu, even though from the reader's perspective such correspondence would in fact, only be internally coherent to the particular Gestalt. This apparent correspondence (which is no real correspondence for the reader), nonetheless remains certain for the ancient Greeks—until, of course, the Comic consciousness discovers the gods of their pantheon are actually human creations and then the entire form (Gestalt) of consciousness and the epistemology associated with it no longer coheres, but instead crumbles, upon such a realization.

From the perspective of the reader it would also be incorrect to replace the word "Gestalt" with the word "coherence" when one is in the context of absolute knowing, because although absolute knowing can be conceived of as a form of consciousness, it does more than just cohere within itself—it also corresponds to the Notion. Recall in his article, "Truth and Self-Satisfaction," Solomon explains that "On the one hand, Hegel sees that isolated beliefs can never be true nor false, for it is by virtue of the *system* of beliefs (desires, practices, etc.) that a particular belief has a world to correspond to. Yet *within* that conception, which Hegel clearly endorses ["The Truth is the Whole" (*Phenomenology of Spirit*, p. 81)], it yet remains true that truth is correspondence. A belief is never true *simply* by virtue of its coherence within our system of beliefs, but by virtue of its coherence *and* correspondence with the facts."³ This quality of truth, which Solomon describes Hegel to hold, must be both internally coherent while corresponding to actual facts about the world. These facts are ascertained in the Hegelian system once absolute knowing is reached. In the final form of consciousness, absolute knowing, the individual has certainty that their knowledge both corresponds to actuality and coheres to the larger body of knowledge they possess. Although this is true for the case of absolute knowing, it cannot be said to be true concerning all the other forms (Gestalten) of Spirit leading up to absolute knowing. These prior forms of Spirit are only coherent in nature, and the fundamental premises that allow these forms to be internally coherent do not correspond to facts (take for example the claims of phrenology or the claims in the Greek religion that the Greek gods in the pantheon have actual existence in themselves). These former shapes of Spirit are coherent ways of knowing primarily. When they do correspond to actuality, Hegel suggest that they do so incompletely. He explains that these ways of knowing still contain implicit contradiction, but that it is just the case that the individuals whose minds belong to such coherence epistemologies have not realized the contradictions latent in the systems. These contradictions are for Hegel and his readers to discover.

If we now consider the idea that the word "coherence" could be conceptually substituted for the word "Gestalt" in the context of the reader with respect to all forms of consciousness except absolute knowing, we begin to understand why Hegel's epistemology can be mistaken for a coherence epistemology, particularly when we consider insightful remarks such as the one Loewenberg makes when commenting on absolute knowing. When evaluating Hegel's claim of absolute knowing, Loewenberg explains,

> Phenomenological relativity of knowledge is the point at issue. Is the relativity assumed or proved? The principle that proof of relativity hinges on prior assumption of absoluteness is one on which the entire phenomenology of mind is grounded: every mode of consciousness makes its appearance with a claim on certainty that cannot be set aside except by immanent criticism. The experience of sense-certainty which starts the dialectical ball rolling is archetypal. All subsequent certainties, such as those relating to self-consciousness, reason, culture, conscience, religion, have their beginning in the assertion of absoluteness only to end as relative to a truth more comprehensive. The notion of

---

3. Solomon, "Truth and Self-Satisfaction," 703.

absolute knowledge, far from being alien to phenomenology, is its very soul and leaven.[4]

In this commentary by Loewenberg we find a few fascinating ideas concerning how to comprehend the series of forms of consciousnesses leading up to absolute knowing. The first interesting description that Loewenberg brings to light in his commentary is that for the consciousness in each stage of the *Phenomenology* (as opposed to the reader observing each of the stages of consciousness) the form of consciousness possesses the quality of being ostensibly absolute. That is, it appears taken for granted that this form of consciousness simply is true. It remains in existence because it remains a satisfactory form of understanding the world for the people participating in its *Volksgeist*. Until, of course, contradictions are discovered, and the way of knowing is superseded by a new form of consciousness, which is able to better manage the contradictions. When the new form of consciousness emerges, one may wonder how the former form passed muster—but it did because it was simply thought to be true. Particular premises (such as sense certainty) were simply the starting points for knowledge—and they were not questioned to the degree necessary to discover the contradiction present in the premise. This is why, as we mentioned earlier, from the perspective of the individual consciousness enveloped within one of the various milieus which Hegel presents, it would not be appropriate to substitute the word "coherence" for the word "Gestalt." Again, this is because for such an individual this inadequate relative form of knowledge has the quality for them of being absolute and more than just coherent. Given the phenomenological data which Hegel provides, an advocate of coherence epistemologies—and by advocate we mean to say a person who argues for the existence of coherence epistemologies—can make a case that coherence epistemologies do exist in actuality.[5]

---

4. Loewenberg, *Hegel's Phenomenology*, 356.

5. Here it is important to consider the distinction between coherentism as a theory of truth vis-à-vis a theory of justification. In his work *Hegelian Metaphysics*, Robert Stern elaborates on such a distinction by explaining that "Coherence as a theory of truth claims that truth consists in, or can be defined as, coherence: that is, a belief is true if and only if it coheres with other beliefs. Coherence as a theory of justification claims that a belief is justified if and only if it forms part of a coherent belief-system. As is often pointed out, these two positions are distinct and separable: for example, one could be a coherentist about justification, while adopting a correspondence theory of truth." Stern, *Hegelian Metaphysics*, 183. If one were to read Hegel's *Phenomenology of Spirit* and not find his description of absolute knowing convincing, one may still be convinced that coherence epistemologies exists. One could also claim that individuals found that their beliefs are

One could arguably claim that Hegel has proven the existence of coherence epistemologies, while at the same time acknowledging that Hegel, himself, does not believe that the manner of knowing in which he ultimately offers his readers is itself a coherent epistemology. Put another way, Hegel outlines what is both convincing and inadequate about various forms of Spirit (*Volksgeist*) he examines. The reader, on the one hand, observes the various *Volksgeist* to serve as satisfactory epistemologies for the people who belong to them, while on the other hand, the reader also observes that these epistemologies lack correspondence to actuality—rendering them only coherent in nature. Hegel attempts to demonstrate to the reader that the concluding form of knowledge, absolute knowing, is not like this because it is void of contradictions, and because, unlike the previous forms of knowledge, it fully corresponds to the Concept. Hegel, although demonstrating—perhaps better than anyone before him—that coherence epistemologies exist, attempts to assure his readers that he is offering them something more than merely a coherence epistemology, when he presents absolute knowing.

The second interesting description which comes out of Loewenberg's comments is the relative aspect of the knowledge that is experienced by the consciousness enveloped in the milieu as absolute. This is intriguing because it dovetails nicely into the earlier discussed criticism of coherence epistemologies which Robert Solomon provided when discussing the implications of Hegel's topsy-turvy world philosophical thought experiment. Recall that Solomon explained that Hegel's critique in this thought experiment was primarily geared toward Kantian epistemology, but that it worked equally as well as a critique of coherence epistemologies because the inverse of every truth claim within a coherence epistemology is equally as coherent—but (we may assume) not equally as true. In the *Phenomenology*, as seen through Loewenberg's comments, one is able to see various coherence epistemologies emerge and ostensibly function as though the knowledge claims which cohere with them are absolute. The reader then observes Hegel bring to light the contradictions in these systems of knowing, and the reader realizes that this Gestalt was not absolute, but rather it was contingent—and therefore the knowledge and the framework which brings forth such knowledge is instead relative. In certain

---

coherent in the system they subscribe to but believe that their coherent set of beliefs corresponds to the way the world actually is. It is these types of systems that Hegel seems to present leading up to absolute knowing. These individuals appear to be coherentist (at best—some merely appear to be dogmatist or absolutist) with respect to justification.

extreme cases the assertions will even be made—as it is by Verene—that the knowledge system is the very inverse, or topsy-turvy version of actual absolute knowing; this is the case, Verene suggests, with phrenology being the inverse of phenomenology.

We can now grasp why an individual may conclude that Hegel has shown proof of the existence of coherence epistemologies—but that this is quite different than saying that Hegel is exclusively advocating a coherence epistemology when he offers absolute knowing as an epistemological system. Quite the opposite appears to be the case. Hegel is offering a method of absolute knowing, one that in theory affords the knower assurance that they are not merely enveloped in a coherence epistemology that although it appears to be internally coherent, may not correspond to anything. Why then would some commentators concluded that Hegel's epistemology is coherent in nature? Again, Loewenberg provides some perspective on a possible answer. After commenting on the relative nature of all forms of knowledge leading up to absolute knowing, Loewenberg asks a question and then provides a tentative answer to it—he writes, "But do the varieties of mind's postures which the treatise depicts add up to absolute completeness? This hypothesis is open to attack on two grounds: premise and conclusion are equally doubtful. Who can seriously maintain that at the end of the phenomenological pilgrimage all human persuasions form an absolute totality requiring for comprehension an absolute spirit? And does it follow that none but the Hegelian Absolute may thus be proved to exist for the purpose of grasping and encompassing in synthesis the dialectical gyrations of mankind's inordinately assertive beliefs? 'Not proven' must of course be the Scotch verdict."[6] Furthermore, Loewenberg writes with equal skepticism about the likelihood that Hegel has discovered the path to absolute knowing, "Is it possible seriously to maintain that the absolute subject of absolute knowledge can be incontrovertibly demonstrated by the dialectical method without ascribing to that method a power almost preternatural? By making or by seeming to make a claim so excessive if not arrogant Hegel greatly detracts from the value of his important insights which the book so richly affords."[7]

It is with these skeptical comments by Loewenberg concerning the unlikeliness that Hegel has delivered on the promise of absolute knowing that we can deduce why some may conclude that Hegel's own

---

6. Loewenberg, *Hegel's Phenomenology*, 362.
7. Loewenberg, *Hegel's Phenomenology*, 365.

epistemology—and in fact the nature of any epistemological system—is coherent in nature. If Hegel has not proven his case, as Loewenberg argues that he has not, then what is the reader to think concerning the system of knowledge which Hegel is claiming is absolute? Is Hegel's system just one more example of a coherent epistemology—much like the many other coherent systems of knowing which preceded it? It may be suggested that if one answers these questions in the affirmative, then one would be inclined to conclude that Hegel's system of knowing is ultimately coherent in nature. This conclusion may also be one of the "important insights which the book so richly affords," as Loewenberg explains. If one concludes as much, one may see Hegel as able to brilliantly point out all the contradictions in every system of thought he encountered except for his own. We get a first-hand account of an individual enveloped in a coherent epistemology—firmly believing his system of knowing is justifiably absolute but unaware that it is merely relative, just as all the other systems of knowledge he has critiqued are. In this situation the three skeptical discoveries manifest themselves with great concern over the necessity of our experience. While remaining agnostic over the nature of things in the current milieu, our aim will be to explore these three skeptical discoveries with respect to the "Religion as a form of Art," because this was the last and most elaborate system that Hegel explored before declaring it relative and moving on to interpret the revealed religion philosophically. We wish to explore how the three skeptical discoveries manifest themselves in this coherent system of knowledge—and examine the point at which there appears to be an indistinguishability between the arbitrary and non-arbitrary nature of things.

Examining Hegel's Portrayal of Ancient Greece in the *Phenomenology*

Hegel provides a rather lengthy analysis of what he considers to be the salient features of ancient Greek life with respect to the Spirit's phenomenology. He does this both in this chapter on Spirit in which he demonstrates the activity of Spirit in the ethical order of ancient Greek society and in his chapter on religion, when he further provides interpretations of Greek life through examining how his idea of self-consciousness relates to a variety of ancient Greek art forms and religious practices. Hegel appears to further suggest that through the discoveries of the inessential or contingent nature of both Greek ethical and religious life, such forms of life were no longer possible in the way they once were. Such forms of life were no longer possible as they formerly were because they were formerly grounded in the idea that such ethics or religious practices were absolute. Ancient Greek society, according to Hegel, goes from experiencing the gods, to experiencing themselves as the creators of such gods. The comic consciousness watches as the various gods which dwell in the pantheon become fewer and fewer in number, until there are none that reside there any longer. We, the reader, observe how many things in ancient Greek society are shown to be arbitrary, throughout the process of the *Phenomenology*. In this chapter, we will examine this process and show how the skepticism in each one of the skeptical discoveries manifest itself in Hegel's presentation of Greek society. After we have demonstrated this, we will then explore whether the same skeptical discoveries apply equally to our contemporary situation. We begin with the first skeptical discovery, namely that there exists a compatibility between what is universal and what is arbitrary.

The Ancient Greek Ethical World: Examining the First Skeptical Discovery

Hegel introduces the reader to the idea of Spirit in a rather complex way, explaining that Spirit is an idea that requires one to grasp it in both the singular and the plural (i.e., plural in the sense that Spirit can divide itself and that its divided aspects can find themselves in contradictory positions to each other), so that one may later attempt to grasp Spirit in its entirety. Hegel explains that "Spirit is the ethical life of a nation in so far as it is the immediate truth—the individual that is in the world."[8] But Hegel also explains that there are various shapes of ethical life for the purpose of the individual to grasp what Spirit is through its activity—and consequently this will also enable the individual to grasp what it itself is, which is also Spirit in and for itself. Explaining the plural aspect of Spirit, Hegel writes, "These shapes, however, are distinguished from the previous ones by the fact that they are real Spirits, actualities in the strict meaning of the word, and instead of being shapes merely of consciousness, are shapes of a world."[9] Although Hegel explains that these shapes are actualities, there are quite a few questions which remain unanswered concerning the nature of things within these "shapes of a world." To begin with, much of the complexity (concerning

---

8. Hegel, *Phenomenology of Spirit*, 265.
9. Hegel, *Phenomenology of Spirit*, 265.

necessity, contingency, and nature) stems from how Hegel describes the nature or necessary activity of Spirit throughout the *Phenomenology*. Spirit seeks to not only manifest itself in the minds of communities of individuals, in a way that both Spirit and the individuals are both in and for themselves, but Spirit also utilizes a particular method in which it seeks to do this. This method is for it to divide itself and to gradually manifest itself more fully in varying degrees, until its totality is observable to individuals such that they can actualize Spirit in themselves.

Given this aforementioned process, ambiguity persists when one attempts to decide whether these shapes of Spirit, or rather, whether Spirits (i.e., Spirit in the plural) are necessary—and whether the things (i.e., the objects, beliefs, practices, rituals, ethics, etc.) of such Spirits are non-arbitrary in nature. One can definitely answer this question in the affirmative—that various Spirits are necessary, and that the things of such Spirits are non-arbitrary in nature. If one does as much one would not be incorrect as long as one is grounding such Spirits' necessity in the overall movement of Spirit (singular) for the express purpose of actualizing the Concept. Put another way, such Spirits are necessary for us, but not in themselves. (However, it still remains unclear whether particular things have non-arbitrary natures, even in reference to the "for us" perspective. It does appear reasonable to conclude that if particular things contribute to the overall movement and presentation of Spirit, then their natures would be non-arbitrary as it relates to the overarching purpose of Spirit to actualize itself.) Likewise, one is justified in claiming that such Spirits are not necessary in themselves, in that they are contingent and do not correspond to the Concept. Given this perspective, the things of such Spirit would be rightly viewed as arbitrary or at the very least contingent.

In the section entitled "The true Spirit. The ethical order." Hegel attempts to provide an example of this dynamic process which is Spirit. He does so by utilizing aspects of ancient Greek ethical life. Here Hegel writes, "The simple substance of Spirit, as consciousness is divided.... But each of these divisions of substance remains Spirit in its entirety; if in sense-perception things have no other substance than the two determinations of individuality and universality, here these determinations express only the superficial antithesis of the two sides."[10] In this quote by Hegel, two quite interesting things are explained. The first is that substance itself is divided into consciousness—and that this consciousness (which is substance) is

---

10. Hegel, *Phenomenology of Spirit*, 267.

experienced as what it is in itself immediately or absolutely. Such consciousness is not aware of the process of Spirit, which has transpired on the part of Spirit, to bring it into being. Concerning this fact, the reader has insight that the consciousness of those being described do not. We also learn that there are "two determinations" of consciousness, and that these determinations are "individuality" and "universality." What Hegel is attempting to convey in a rather complicated manner is that Spirit is both "individual" and "universal" in nature, but that the only way to have a human mind grasp this dynamic nature (a human mind in the position of Hegel's reader for example) is for Spirit to divide itself into both the "individual consciousness" and the "universal consciousness." This is done so that the reader becomes aware of, first the distinction between the two consciousnesses; then the reader becomes aware of the contradictions which would ensue, and finally the reader would become aware of a new form of consciousness which has reconciled the aforementioned contradiction. In order for the human mind to grasp any of this, however, all of these distinctions, contradictions and resolutions, according to Hegel, must be actualized.[11] And it is in Hegel's presentation of the actualizing process within ancient Greek ethical life, that the question of whether the nature of such things actualized are arbitrary or non-arbitrary becomes an issue.

Concerning these two forms of consciousness, Hegel explains that they are actualized in the human and divine law, and in men and women respectively. The actualization process can be understood as follows: The universal consciousness is actualized in the human law of the ancient Greek ethical world and it is actualized in the nature of men in that world, and the individual consciousness is actualized in the divine law of the ancient Greek ethical world and in the nature of women in that world. This distinctions between the two forms of consciousness are also maintained by the institutions of government which enforces the universal consciousness and of family, which enforces the particular consciousness.

---

11. It is somewhat unclear what Hegel ultimately means by "actualization" because many of Hegel's examples find their inspiration in the literature which Hegel is familiar with. What remains unclear is whether Hegel believed that such literature was indicative of a form of consciousness actualized in real people—and that it was simply better for didactic purposes to utilizes the examples in literature—or whether it was rather the case that Hegel found that concrete examples in literature were a sufficient enough example of an aspect of Spirit, for his reader to grasp such particular various aspects leading up to grasping the totality of Spirit.

Concerning the institution of the family, Hegel explains, "The positive End peculiar to the Family is the individual as such."[12]

Now Hegel's reader, we imagine, sees the nature of all such things in this ancient Greek ethical life quite differently than the individuals who are in this particular form of Spirit (i.e., one of the many forms of Spirit or "shapes of a world"). To his reader, Hegel explains that "these two universal beings of the ethical world [i.e., man and woman] have, therefore, their specific individuality in naturally distinct self-consciousnesses, because the ethical Spirit is the immediate unity of the substance with self-consciousness—an immediacy which appears, therefore, both from the side of reality and of difference, as the existence of a natural difference."[13] His readers now grasp (according to what Hegel has just now described) how this actualization of the consciousnesses of both men and women in ancient Greek ethical life, are phenomenologically experienced: They are experienced as natural, immediate, universal, and non-arbitrary. From the reader's perspective, however, the natural, non-arbitrary nature of such actualization can, in fact be questioned. Farneth, for example, in her work *Hegel's Social Ethics* describes this dual perspective (i.e., that of the reader digesting Hegel's insights about Greek *Sittlichkeit*, as opposed to the experience of both male and female enveloped in the milieu of ancient Greek ethical life) when she explains, "It is not nature but the ethical norms of that shape of spirit that determine which laws apply to which people, even though the members of Greek *Sittlichkeit* do not recognized this. On their view, nature dictates which law applies to each person depending on his or her sex. Therefore, each ethical consciousness, male or female, takes one of the ethical powers, the human law or the divine law, as determining his or her obligations. The result is that men and women experience themselves as having distinct identities and obligations, each exclusive of and opposed to the other."[14]

Given this difference of perspective between those reading Hegel's presentation of the phenomenological experience of ancient Greek ethical life, and those Hegel describes as experiencing this particular phenomenological experience from within this particular form of Spirit, let us further examine each one of these aspects which are phenomenologically experienced, i.e., the naturalness, the immediacy, the universality and the non-arbitrariness which make up this particular phenomenological

---

12. Hegel, *Phenomenology of Spirit*, 269.
13. Hegel, *Phenomenology of Spirit*, 276.
14. Farneth, *Hegel's Social Ethics*, 19.

experience. Hegel states that the immediacy, which is the "unity of substance with self-consciousness," makes such a difference, between the two forms of consciousnesses, appear as though it were a "natural difference." This feature is distinct, phenomenologically speaking according to Hegel, from other forms of ethical consciousnesses, such as the "Legal Status," found in ancient Roman society, and which, the *Phenomenology* describes as emerging from the Greek ethical life. With "Legal Status," one would have a very different phenomenological experience of what both grounds and obligates one to behave ethically. The laws, with respect to "Legal Status," are not something that are natural, but rather they are a product of the Roman legal system. Citizenship is also something that is not understood to be necessarily natural or immediate, but rather it is socially constructed, often mediated by a process, possesses a historical context, and could be acquired by other means than birth. Furthermore, in "Legal Status," the ethical laws of citizens were universal in that they applied to all citizens, but they were not universal in the sense that not all people under the Roman Empire were citizens of the Roman Empire.

With this contrast, we observe how Greek *Sittlichkeit* appeared natural, universal, and non-arbitrary, given its immediacy, but we also observe that from the perspective of the reader, Greek *Sittlichkeit* was a product of either social construction, or a movement of the Spirit, and because of this perspective it appears arbitrary from the reader's point of view. We also observe that—given Hegel's description—in the milieu of ancient Greece, such distinctions in ethical consciousnesses between man and woman also appeared universal. (Again, this is not to say that historically this was the case—but rather that this appears implicit in Hegel's description of what he believes to be the case.) This appearance of universality of such a distinction of consciousnesses, coupled with—from the reader's perspective—the arbitrary nature of such a distinction, provides us with an exemplification of our first skeptical discovery, i.e., that what is universal and what is arbitrary can be compatible. Here we have an actualized example of the doubt of this very skeptical discovery manifested in ancient Greek ethical life. From the reader's perspective it is merely arbitrary that Spirit divided itself in the manner that it did—everything could have just as well been topsy-turvy. For example, although throughout the *Phenomenology* two essential aspects of Spirit—individuality and universality—appear to be a necessary form for Spirit to divide into, so that the human mind can ultimately understand Spirit; the way in which this necessary division actualizes itself appears arbitrary from the reader's standpoint. The particular milieu in which it is actualized appears arbitrary, as does the particularities of the milieu. Speaking again to the possibility of the topsy-turvy aspect of the situation, the reader wonders why it was necessary for Spirit to assign and actualized the ethical universality to the human law and the ethical particularity to the divine law; and further why, likewise to assign to woman and to family the divine law, and to government and to man the human law. Could not the actualization of the nature of any one of these things (from the perspective of Spirit, which the reader is beginning to grasp) just as easily been its inverse? The first skeptical discovery answers this question in the affirmative.

Recall, that although the topsy-turvy world thought-experiment, according to Solomon and others, was primarily aimed at critiquing the Kantian epistemological point of view, Solomon explained that it can equally serve as a critique of coherence epistemologies. We can likewise now observe how this philosophical thought-experiment can serve equally well as a critique of the certainty of the particular milieu or Gestalt of ancient Greek ethical life. This is because the situation which Hegel has created for the ancient Greeks is quite similar to the situation which Kant created for his audience in one respect. Kant, as we know, designed an epistemological gap between the phenomenal and the noumenal world. Hegel, throughout the *Phenomenology*, has done a similar thing—or rather expressed a similar type of situation—for all peoples enveloped in the various milieus or forms of Spirit in the history he describes. (This applies to all people living prior to the point where this philosophical history has completed itself and absolute knowing is possible for those who are able to observe the movements of Spirit in its entirety.) Such individuals are not in a milieu in which Spirit has actualized itself, in a manner in which it is in itself and for itself, but rather they are in a shape of the world—so to speak—in which Spirit has divided itself for the benefit of the later observer. For such individuals there exists a similar epistemological gap between their phenomenological experience, in which Spirit actualizes itself for us (i.e., Hegel and his readers) as well as in them, and Spirit actualizing itself in and for itself. Although such individuals take their phenomenological experiences to be absolute, they, in reality, have no way of knowing for sure that things are not actually the inverse of what they phenomenologically appear to be.

Why do such individuals never suspect such lack of certainty? There are essentially two distinct answers to this question (though these two answers can overlap). The first answer is provided by Hegel explicitly, and the second answer is our first skeptical discovery, which we argue is implicit in Hegel's topsy-turvy world thought-experiment. The answer provided by Hegel is that individuals will continue to see such aspects of their world as absolute and non-arbitrary until a contradiction arises in their particular world (a contradiction which is momentous in nature—and even if the contradiction is momentous, sometimes individuals of the particular Volksgeist, it stands to reason, may not recognize the contradiction as a contradiction). In the ancient Greek ethical order, this contradiction arises, according to Hegel, in the conflict between Antigone and Creon over the ethical correctness of Antigone burying her brother. In the Hegelian interpretation of this conflict, Antigone is naturally obligated to obey the divine law, whereas Creon is naturally obligated to obey the human law—and in this particular circumstance the divine law and the human law contradict each other. This contradiction demonstrates the incompleteness of ancient Greek ethical life, as well as the inadequacies of the corresponding divisions of Spirit.

The second answer to this question is the first skeptical discovery, which suggests that individuals will remain unaware of the arbitrary nature of something as long as the nature of the thing appears universal. The example that Hegel is most fond of utilizing when describing the topsy-turvy world thought-experiment is the example of salt. Salt, Hegel explains, phenomenologically speaking, is white, and cubical, and bitter, but for all we know could have the very opposite properties in the noumenal or topsy-turvy world. The reason we do not normally question such properties, however, is because there is universality (or at least general consensus) of phenomenological experiences pertaining to such things. If, however, there were an absence of universal consensus of experience such that experience varied widely with great statistical significance, then the assumed non-arbitrary nature of the thing would be called into question. Likewise, in ancient Greek society, if there was not universality (or strong general consistency) between such things as the human law, government, and the nature of man, or between divine law, family, and the nature of woman—but rather such associations oscillated capriciously each day; it would then be evident to all that what formerly was taken to be the non-arbitrary nature of such things, were in fact merely arbitrary.

Fate in the Ancient Greek World: An Examination of the Second Skeptical Discovery

In this section we aim to show how fate (much like phrenology) serves to exemplify our second skeptical discovery/worry. This second skeptical discovery acknowledges that the existence of coherence epistemologies make determinations concerning the degree to which one's system of reasoning bears any resemblance to actuality a matter of uncertainty. Given this aim, there are a few passages in the *Phenomenology* which we will be examining in this section. We will begin by reviewing how Hegel explains Reason relating to Spirit (in para. 438). We find this review particularly valuable because as we compare the former insights which we obtained while considering phrenology in the context of coherence epistemologies, with the insights we hope to obtain considering fate in the context of coherence epistemologies—we want to be perfectly clear concerning how Reason relates to Spirit. In this section we also aim to examine how Hegel sees the general idea of fate relating to phrenology. In addition to this we will be discussing how Hegel understands fate to be exemplified in ancient Greek culture, in his comments on the story of Oedipus and how this exemplification embodies the doubt found in the second skeptical discovery.

Let us begin by examining how Hegel explains Reason relating to Spirit. At the beginning of his chapter on Spirit, Hegel states that "Reason is Spirit when its certainty of being all reality has been raised to truth, and it is consciousness of itself as its own world, and of the world as itself."[15] What this description explains is that Reason can be properly understood as Spirit when Reason is actualized in a form of Spirit or shape of the world in such a way that it is phenomenologically experienced to be comprehensive (i.e., not lacking due to contradictions) and absolute, with respect to the particular reality of a particular world. Given this explanation, fate appears to be a form of Reason that can be understood as Spirit (in the context of Religion) because as Hegel presents this phenomenon in ancient Greek culture, it appears to be taken as both comprehensive and absolute—such as in the story of Oedipus. Phrenology, likewise, although presented in the chapter on Reason, can, in the context of its milieu be understood as Spirit, contributing to an overall understanding of a particular form of Spirit. This is to say that both Fate and phrenology (respectively) contribute to the overall coherence of a particular form of Spirit which they are a part

---

15. Hegel, *Phenomenology of Spirit*, 263.

of. This is evident because there is a particular community of individuals in a particular milieu during the time of Hegel that have subscribed to the particular form of reasoning (i.e., a coherent aspect of a form of Spirit) found or exemplified in phrenology—and such Reason appears to those who hold it to be comprehensive and absolute. In his section discussing physiognomy and phrenology, Hegel addresses the general idea of fate through his comparison of palmistry with phrenology and physiognomy. Hegel initially explains that palmistry is different from phrenology and physiognomy because the former does not consider "specific individuality in the necessary antithesis of an inner and an outer, of character as a conscious disposition, and this again as an existent shape, and the way it relates these factors to each other is the way they are related by their Notion."[16] Hegel then contrasts this characterizations of relating the internal with the external (which he finds indicative of phrenology and physiognomy) with other practices that relate what he refers to as "an outer to an outer." It is here that Hegel addresses palmistry as one such practice, and in addressing palmistry, he addresses the idea of fate. Concerning the relation of palmistry to fate, Hegel explains that "these particular lines on the hand are external factors indicating a longer or shorter life and the fate in general of the particular individual."[17] The example of the lines on the hands serve as one of the external factors (or as an "outer" as Hegel describes it) and for a moment Hegel also appears to view the particular person's fate likewise, i.e., as the second external factor. This view of fate reinforces Hegel's idea of palmistry being different in kind from phrenology and physiognomy, because it relates an "outer with an outer."

Surprisingly enough, however, Hegel changes his position on palmistry, and in so doing provides the reader with a more detailed understanding of his general view of fate, explaining "admittedly the hand does not seem to be such a very external factor for fate; it seems rather to be related to it as something inner. For fate itself is also only the manifestation of what the particular individuality is in itself as an inner original specific character."[18] Before proceeding to how Hegel views fate as it relates to ancient Greek culture in the stories relating to Oedipus and Antigone, a few relevant questions concerning fate emerge from this description as it relates to the second skeptical discovery. The first question is whether a concept such as fate

16. Hegel, *Phenomenology of Spirit*, 188.
17. Hegel, *Phenomenology of Spirit*, 188.
18. Hegel, *Phenomenology of Spirit*, 188.

corresponds to anything in actuality—i.e., it is the question of whether there is actually an "in itself" which pertains to "what the particular individuality is?" The second question is, if we suppose an affirmative answer to the first question—that fate, in actuality, is "the manifestation of what the particular individuality is in itself," then what practices or systems of knowledge provide access to the knowledge of what a particular person's fate is? In the example just now provided of palmistry, an affirmative answer is provided for the first question, and palmistry is provided as the answer to the second question. In ancient Greek culture, an affirmative is also provided for the first question, and the idea of an oracle, who can provide individuals with information concerning the fate of a particular person (such as in the story of Oedipus), is the answer to the second question.

Hegel discusses fate with respect to the ancient Greek milieu, in the section titled, "Ethical action. Human and Divine Knowledge. Guilt and Destiny." In this section, Hegel examines how fate operates in an individual who is not aware of the ethical gravity of his crime (Oedipus) as well as an individual who is aware of the gravity of her crime (Antigone). Concerning the former, Hegel writes, "Actuality therefore holds conceded within it the other aspect which is alien to this knowledge and does not reveal the whole truth about itself to consciousness: the son does not recognize his father in the man who has wronged him and whom he slays, nor his mother in the queen who he makes his wife."[19] In this case we observe a fate which is "actuality" and internal to Oedipus, concealing itself from his consciousness—and here one can only presume had the truth been revealed to Oedipus prior to him committing such acts that he would have refrained from committing them, and what was his fate would not have been actualized; whereas had Oedipus's fate not been revealed to his parents, one can only presume that his fate would likewise not have been actualized. Fate, however, being actual and the inner aspect of the particular individual, reveals and conceals itself for the purpose of its own actualization. With Hegel's interpretation of the story of Oedipus, we observe both types of fatalism—as van Inwagen describes them[20] manifested for the purpose of the particular fate being actualized.

19. Hegel, *Phenomenology of Spirit*, 283.

20. In his work *An Essay on Free Will*, van Inwagen describes two different types of Fatalism. Distinguishing the one from the other he writes, "Suppose a witch predicts that I shall drown within the next twenty-four hours. She also predicts that I shall attempt to evade this fate, and that my efforts will be in vain. Here are two stories about how her prediction might come true. (a) I determine to spend the next twenty-four hours at the

The case of Antigone is somewhat different according to Hegel, because she is already aware of both the human law and the divine law. She is also aware that when she obeys the divine law, which she knows that she will, such obedience will involve breaking the human law, and that this breaking of the law will be a crime that she will be guilty of. Hegel explains that this situation is the case for Antigone when he writes, "But the ethical consciousness is more complete, its guilt more inexcusable, if it knows beforehand the law and the power which it opposes, if it takes them to be violence and wrong, to be ethical merely by accident, and, like Antigone, knowingly commits the crime."[21] Here, however, fate, although present in the actions of Antigone and Creon, is not as much emphasized as it is in their mutual downfall—and in this mutual downfall the incompleteness in each ethical form of consciousness is illustrated. It is in assuring the downfall of each side that Hegel sees fate's activity to be. Concerning such downfall, he writes, "Only in the downfall of both sides alike is absolute right accomplished, and the ethical substance as the negative power which engulfs both sides, that is, omnipotent and righteous Destiny, steps on the scene."[22]

We can observe, given the description of fate in ancient Greek society, how it would be difficult to determine with any certainty, whether such a way of knowing corresponded with any form of actuality (meaning it would be difficult to determine whether it is the case that we all in fact have a Destiny which is inescapable). If one were not in the position of the reader, but rather in the particular milieu where both the idea of fate, and the practice of learning of one's particular fate were seen as unchallenged certainties of this particular milieu, one can observe the difficulty in determining whether such a customary way of knowing could be determined to correspond

---

top of a high hill. But as I leave the witch's hovel, I am overpowered by three assailants in the employ of an enemy of mine, who, despite my struggles, carry me to a nearby pond and hold me under water till I am dead. (b) I determine to spend the next twenty-four hours at the top of a high hill. While climbing the hill, I fall into a hidden well and drown. Moreover, if I had simply gone about my business and done nothing in particular to avoid drowning, I should not have drowned." Van Inwagen, *An Essay on Free Will*, 23.

21. Hegel, *Phenomenology of Spirit*, 284.

22. Concerning how this phrase relates to the various gods in the Greek pantheon, Loewenberg explains that "the 'depopulation of Heaven', as Hegel calls it, the ultimate expulsion of separate and independent deities, begins in tragedy, Zeus alone emerging as the acknowledged being from which everything derives its destiny.... In tragedy proper, however, precisely because of his strangeness and aloofness, Zeus is simply synonymous with the abstract principle of necessity and destiny, indeed, no distinction can be drawn relating to tragic action." Loewenberg, *Hegel's Phenomenology*, 330.

to actuality. We can observe, too, the independence of the former question from that of the latter question. The former merely questions the actuality of fate, whereas the latter pertains to the methods available for discerning the particular fate of an individual. If one does not believe in the actuality of fate, then any method for obtaining information concerning ones fate would he considered arbitrary. If one, however, believes in the actuality of the former, then particular methods concerning obtaining information about the fate of individuals could still be considered doubtful. An example of this case would be an individual during the time of Hegel, believing in fate via palmistry, but at the same time finding the fundamental premises which cohere the ancient Greek system of knowledge concerning fate less than compelling. In this situation one would find the oracle's association with accurate knowledge concerning one's fate completely arbitrary—and although such an idea of an oracle may satisfactorily cohere within the particular system in question, it does not correspond in any way to actuality. Recall that a parallel type of case has already been examined earlier in this manuscript regarding the underlying premise which links ways of understanding such as phrenology, behaviorism, neurophysiology and genetics. Recall that such premises were that mentality was both generalizable and thoroughly accessible to external observation. The particular method of seeking access to mentality changes over the centuries, from phrenology, to behaviorism, to neurophysiology and genetics, but the fundamental belief in the aforementioned premises persists.

As a new method arises, the former method is viewed as corresponding less to actuality than it once did. Concerning why individuals and communities persist in believing in the more fundamental beliefs is unclear. Hegel, himself, never offers us an answer to this, but answers could range from individuals and communities not being able to systematically cohere a reality that is drastically different from the current one, to other possible answers such as an awareness of the fundamental nature of certain beliefs to particular realities, and given this awareness, the belief becomes too important to challenge.[23] Following the phenomenological dialectical path which

23. Here I am reminded of many of the commentaries on the work of anthropologist Evans-Pritchard, as well as his own thoughts, when reflecting on the persistence of the beliefs of the Azande people concerning the existence and efficacy of witchcraft. For example, Daniel Pals writes, "the fundamental assumptions of the Zande world view are very well protected against facts that might disprove them; indeed, they form a system of beliefs impossible to shake. From our perspective the Azande may be wrong, but from theirs it is clear that they think quite rationally within the limits their culture chooses to

Hegel provides, we can assume that affirmative answers to the first question, and the belief in the efficacy of the oracle providing information concerning an individual's fate, are met with greater skepticism upon the advent of the comic consciousness. The comic consciousness, relating to the art form of poetry and the genre of comedy, brings with it the realization that the gods (and by implication, the oracle of the gods) are merely the creation of human (the ancient Greek community) self-consciousness. The comic consciousness, according to Hegel, is the consciousness in which this realization occurs, but it is the unhappy consciousness in which the implications of this realization are fully felt. Concerning this situation, Hegel applies the expression "God is dead," to describe the loss felt by this consciousness. This loss is the loss of "all essential being in this certainty of itself, and of the loss even of this knowledge about itself—the loss of substance as well as of the self."[24] This is the loss that occurs, according to Hegel, when the gods of the Greek pantheon are discovered to no longer have intrinsic being, but rather merely have their being in the self, which is human. This is a realization that all essential associations of things involving such gods are now met with doubt concerning whether such associations bear any correspondence to actuality. Through his presentation of ancient Greek society, Hegel shows us the phenomenological process in which particular certainties are made into uncertainties. From the reader's perspective, we are able to look upon the phenomenological stage in which there was certainty with respect to fate, and we are able to consider the uncertainty which will later manifest with the advent of the comic consciousness. The example of this perspective that the reader has, concerning such aforementioned certainty, illustrates the worry of the second skeptical discovery. The worry concerns how we are to know if a coherent system, and the ways of knowing thereof, bear any correspondence to actuality.[25]

---

allow. Their small beliefs rest very logically on certain larger ones, and these important basic principles are extremely well guarded. The attachment to the major beliefs is so fundamental to their life that the Azande cannot imagine them to be in error. Without them, their entire social order would be inconceivable, and no one could endure that. As students of contemporary culture have come to realize, what Evans-Pritchard shows to be true for the Azande holds consequences for the assessment of belief and doubt in our own social circumstances. The case of the Azande suggests that in any culture, certain fundamental beliefs *must* at all costs be preserved; they are too precious and crucial to lose." Pals, *Nine Theories of Religion*, 273.

24. Hegel, *Phenomenology of Spirit*, 455.

25. To clarify matters a bit further, if we consider a "correspondence to actuality" within Hegelian ontology, then all phenomena have correspondence to actuality in that

The Mind Which Possesses Absolute Knowing: An Examination of the Third Skeptical Discovery

The phrase "God is dead," is a phrase that is most commonly attributed to Nietzsche's Madman. Prior to the rant of Nietzsche's Madman, Hegel utilized this phrase in a much nuanced way—a way that is relevant to our third skeptical discovery. In the final section of "Religion as a form of Art," Hegel analyzes "The spiritual work of art"; this form of art is Greek poetry, which Hegel finds the movement of the Spirit proceeding from epic, to tragedy, to comedy. The result of comedy is the comic consciousness, in which a "comic atheism,"[26] is produced, and a general skepticism for not just the existence of the gods, but for nearly all aspects of ancient Greek society is produced. Concerning the pervasive skepticism, Loewenberg writes, "Scepticism of the gods is not the only result that must be laid at the door of comedy. Ideals and values previously acknowledged and honored are abandoned to scorn and ridicule. The ancient faiths are shown to be delusions, and the ancestral hopes, fictions. All traditional ideas and beliefs, such in particular as relate to the beautiful and the good, now come to be exposed as idols and surrendered to the vulgar as objects to be laughed at."[27] It is to this situation that Hegel applies the phrase "God is dead."

Although Hegel borrows this common phrase from aspects of Lutheran theology at his time, when he utilizes it to apply to how he observes the ancient Greek situation, the meaning of this phrase immediately changes.[28] There are, however, some analogues elements between what Hegel (as

---

they all correspond in some sense to the movement of Spirit. However, in this context a "correspondence to actuality" is referring to the manifestation or actualization of Spirit in-and-for-itself. In this sense, all former movements of Spirit would not correspond to actuality (in this full sense of the term) because these forms of Spirit have not manifested Spirit in-and-for-itself.

26. The term "comic atheism," is a reference to Loewenberg's terminology. When describing this situation he explains, "Be that as it may, what I find disconcerting is the difficulty of squaring comic atheism with the theological anthropomorphism of the religion of art." Loewenberg, *Hegel's Phenomenology*, 332.

27. Loewenberg, *Hegel's Phenomenology*, 332.

28. It is furthermore, unclear whether we should even view the phrase "God is dead" to indicate a monotheistic concept when applied to the ancient Greek situation. For example, because the process of the depopulation of the gods in the pantheon takes place—this takes place phenomenologically in the Greek psyche as Greeks interact with the poetry of tragedy—this phrase can definitely apply to this entire process of depopulation. At the same time, it can be argued that the apex of this process results for a time in only one God remaining—this God being Zeus, with qualities of omnipotence being

interpreted by Loewenberg) is suggesting has occurred in ancient Greek society after the death of God, so to speak, and what Nietzsche's Madman is suggesting has occurred in his milieu, despite the fact that he has "come too early," and the people remain aloof to all that has been affected by the death of God. The parallel we can draw from both situations, is that in both realities, what is being described is that fundamental beliefs that structure a Gestalt of Spirit (i.e., a coherence epistemology) have been sufficiently undermined by doubts to the extent that the system is no longer able to exist as it once did. The divine, which was taken to be absolute, and all the other beliefs, values, and practices associated with such former absolute truth begins to disintegrate. The situation which Hegel presents to the reader concerning the phenomenological situation in ancient Greece, is strikingly similar to the concerns which are provoked by the third skeptical discovery. We observe Hegel's presentation of a people whose understanding of the divine thoroughly informs the structure of their minds. This particular Spirit, which is the substance of their self-consciousness, is not absolute, but rather, though it appears absolute it is an arbitrary creation of their own minds. To make matters more complicated, the reader also observes that such individuals, before the advent of the comic consciousness, do not believe themselves to be the authors of the gods, nor the author of the god's mentality, which then serves to structure and cohere their own mentality. These individuals, prior to the comic consciousness remain aloof to this dynamic process, which is the true structure of their self-consciousness.

The reader, after being introduced to this epistemological situation wonders whether this situation could likewise be the situation that Hegel, and the readers he has convinced, are also in—unbeknownst to them, of course (This is the situation of the third skeptical discovery). The third skeptical discovery questions how we know Hegel has provided us with actual knowledge of the divine mind, as opposed to merely providing us with access to a form of self-consciousness, which is the product of his own creation. The first skeptical discovery demonstrates that we cannot rely on universality or the universal acceptance of such a form of self-consciousness because it is possible for what is universal to be compatible with what is arbitrary. The second skeptical discovery cautions us to accept a system of reasoning simply because it is coherent; this discovery has demonstrated that what is internally coherent can in fact be the opposite or inverse of what actually,

---

ascribed to him. In this case the phrase "God is dead," could be applied monotheistically, but with respect to Zeus.

in fact, is. The third skeptical discovery demonstrates an epistemological option to us (Hegel's reader), one that we ourselves, though in a different milieu, could share with the ancient Greeks. If it were the case that we were in a similar epistemological situation as what Hegel describes the ancient Greeks as being in prior to the comic consciousness—the nature of things in this Gestalt of Spirit would phenomenologically appear non-arbitrary, but in reality, would be arbitrary. We would experience an indistinguishability between the arbitrary and non-arbitrary nature of things.

Hegel desires that his reader find assurance in the final form of Spirit found in the revealed religion of Christianity. Hegel philosophically analyzes this form of Spirit such that he raises the "picture thinking" which is present in its many revealed narratives into conceptual thinking. This analysis, Hegel found, when paired with the summary of the movement of Spirit, which he provides in his last chapter, was sufficient to demonstrate to the reader that the result of working through the *Phenomenology*, is absolute knowing. Once absolute knowing is then achieved, it would inform the reader in such a way that they could distinguish arbitrary nature from non-arbitrary nature with respect to things. The worry, however, is that when all three skeptical discoveries are jointly considered, they provoke sufficient doubt concerning Hegel's conclusion. The reader is left in an agnostic state in which the arbitrary and non-arbitrary nature of things appear to be equally likely possibilities.

A Brief Coda concerning an Alternative to Madness

The failure of Nietzsche's presentation of the Madman, it seems, is that the Madman was never challenged with a formidable dialogue that responded to his rant in a critical way. Let us now imagine the Hegelian agnostic among the crowd of people in the marketplace as the Madman's rant comes to an abrupt end. When this Madman, concludes his rant, would we not expect the Hegelian agnostic to apply an equipollence method[29] reminiscent

---

29. Here I am referring to equipollence in the way in which Forster, in his work *Hegel's Idea of a Phenomenology of Spirit*, understands Hegel to see its significance in the ancient Pyrrhonist, and further how this method takes on significance for Hegel's project of the *Phenomenology*. Equipollence is the method which the ancient Pyrrhonist employed to show that given two disparate conclusions, each was equally likely. This tentative result would therefore cast equal doubt on both conclusions. Concerning this method, Forster describes Hegel as explaining that "the great strength of ancient skepticism lies in its possession of the method of equipollence [*isostheneia*—literally, 'equal force on

of Hegel's interpretation of the ancient skeptics? Would we not expect this agnostic to notice in the Madman's proclamation of the death of God, as well as all the fantastic descriptions which followed, a tone of absolutism? When speaking this rant, the Madman merely finds himself certain about the very claims the crowed remains aloof to. Would not the agnostic simply turn the premises of the Madman's questions into questions themselves, and ask, so to speak, "Have we killed God?" "Do not the possibilities that we have and we have not appear equally as likely?" How might we go about determining whether we have or have not killed God? This question is an interesting way of asking how we might go about assuring ourselves that the nature of things are either arbitrary or non-arbitrary.

In the remaining chapter we will look at ways in which a groundwork can be established so that this question can receive a viable answer. We have, so far, provided a framework, which we found from within the *Phenomenology*, to question the validity of the non-arbitrary nature of things. This framework, or method, however, was so far, only applied to the theoretical and historical material presented in the *Phenomenology*. In this final chapter we aim to apply this method to phenomena in our contemporary world in a manner which highlights the aspect of indistinguishability, with respect to arbitrary and non-arbitrary nature. There are two avenues in which we suggest that the indistinguishability between the arbitrary and non-arbitrary nature of things obtains cogency. The first is to address phenomena which cast doubt on the non-arbitrary nature of things. The second is to explore wide ranging forms of phenomenal experiences which vary significantly, but have possible methods for being universal. The second technique essentially allows us to imagine how varied phenomenological experiences of our world can be. This technique serves to question whether there is, in fact, any non-arbitrary nature necessitating our phenomenological experience to be as it is. The contemporary phenomena we will be exploring in the following chapter are the placebo effect and the use of sensoriums in the field of phenomenological anthropology.

---

both sides'] that is, the method of setting into opposition equally strong propositions or arguments on both sides of any issue that arises, and thereby producing an equal balance of justification on both sides of the issue." Furthermore, Forster writes concerning the ancient skeptics, "For the whole point of the ancient skeptic's procedure of adducing propositions or arguments on both sides of an issue was that he and his audience should find those on neither side more convincing than those on the other." Forster, *Hegel's Idea of a Phenomenology of Spirit*, 129–31.

5

Examining the Cogency of Indistinguishability through the Phenomena of Sensoriums and the Placebo Effect

WE NOW TURN AWAY from a direct reflection on the content of Hegel's *Phenomenology*, to an examination of contemporary phenomena, which perhaps exemplifies the results of a position of epistemological agnosticism that one can—but does not necessarily have to—take concerning the arbitrary nature of things. It is our belief that Hegel has presented, through his descriptions of the various world religions, and particularly with the religion of Ancient Greece, an epistemological situation which shares certain qualities to the situation many cultural anthropologists find themselves in today. It would be a mistake to think that the ontological beliefs or metaphysical positions of Hegel and contemporary anthropologists are shared. Rather what is shared is an attempt to describe a *Volksgeist* or a "shape of a particular Spirit of a people" so to speak, which is not shared by the person describing it. Whereas Hegel's reasons for such descriptions of Spirits are quite different from those of cultural anthropologists, as are his interpretations of such descriptions, the fact remains despite such differences, that a variety of coherence epistemologies, (i.e., differences in *Volksgeists*) produce significant differences in ontologies. The most significant question, which stems from this fact, we find, is, "How should these varieties of ontologies be understood in relation to each other?" We ascertain that the groundwork which Hegel supplies, coupled with the three skeptical discovers suggest a compelling case for epistemological agnosticism regarding the nature of things when we observe how sensoriums are being used in phenomenological and cultural anthropology.

With respect to the way in which the Hegelian system itself functions, such that it leads the reader to absolute knowing through the process of comprehending the movements of Spirit throughout history, we find a similar type of epistemological uncertainty of this process to be shared with the uncertainty presented in a placebo test trial. As Hegel describes the various forms of Spirits of the various religions of the world, the reader observes how the individual who is part of the particular *Volksgeist*, which the reader is reading about, is deceived in trusting that their phenomenological experience corresponds to actuality in any ultimate sense. The reader sees that phenomenological experience both can and cannot be a reliable indicator of actuality. If the reader were in the situation of the individual that the reader is reading about, the reader would have to admit that they would be unable to trust that their phenomenological experiences correspond to actuality (in any ultimate sense). We find that an analogous situation exists for the individual participating in a placebo test trial, because an epistemological agnosticism is requited throughout the entire trial as a necessary condition of the test—it is a necessary epistemological condition of the participant for the results of the trial to be legitimate.

Many times, throughout the *Phenomenology*, Hegel describes Spirit as splitting into two contrary forms. One form of which Spirit will continue its movements through, while the other forms appears merely to exist as an antithesis of the former, so that the contradictions of the former can be comprehended. We find an analogous situation in that of the placebo test trials, in which the experimenter splits the treatment into that which is understood to be arbitrary (the placebo) and that which is understood to be non-arbitrary (the medicine or treatment being tested in the trial) in hopes of demonstrating that the non-arbitrary treatment is in fact non-arbitrary. This situation remains analogous to the Hegelian system, we find, until one questions the non-arbitrariness of the condition or illness itself, which is being treated. Once this questioning occurs, we argue that the position of epistemological agnosticism suggests itself with respect to both illness and treatment. We argue that an analogous situation occurs within the Hegelian system, with the introduction of the three skeptical discovers. We not only use the epistemological situation of the placebo test trial as analogous to the epistemological situation that we argue the Hegelian system results in after the three skeptical discoveries, but we also find that the phenomenon of the placebo/nocebo effect adds credence to the thesis that there is an indistinguishability between the arbitrary and

EXAMINING THE COGENCY OF INDISTINGUISHABILITY

non-arbitrary nature of things. The Hegelian system allows us to apprehend how such arbitrariness can exist with respect to illness and treatment, even in a coherence epistemology in which a non-arbitrariness of illness and treatment is assumed to be the case.

In this chapter we examine two contemporary phenomena with the aim of adding credence to the thesis that there is an indistinguishability between the arbitrary nature and the non-arbitrary nature of things. When we explain that these phenomena add credence to such indistinguishability, as opposed to demonstrate that such indistinguishability exists, it is because we acknowledge that it seems quite counterintuitive to assume such indistinguishability in all things. Although we suggest that this can philosophically be the case, and that an epistemological agnosticism concerning this matter is an appropriate philosophical stance to take after acknowledging the three skeptical discoveries in Hegel's *Phenomenology*, we are aware that the counterintuitive aspect of such a claim persists, and that merely examining two phenomena can only add some credence to this philosophical stance. It would take a reconsideration of much more contemporary phenomena than the two contemporary phenomena we are now considering—and such reconsiderations are beyond the scope of this manuscript. We do suggest that the next contemporary phenomena to examine in relation to the thesis of this manuscript would be synesthesia, and perhaps multi-modal sensory experiences that debatably cannot be illusory, such as the multi-modal experience of flavor. The two contemporary phenomena we will now examine are the utilization of sensoriums in the field of phenomenological anthropology and the placebo effect.

With respect to the first phenomenon—the utilization of sensoriums in the field of phenomenological anthropology—we aim to examine an ethnography in which sensoriums are frequently utilized to provide insight into ways of viewing phenomena as empirically real. Such phenomena may be generally placed within the context of *vodu* as well as the religious activities of the religion of *vodu*. Such phenomena include mysterious illness and spontaneous recovery from illness, malicious entities, and the experience of Nyigbla—the god of lightning. The position of cultural anthropology—following the insights and contributions of Evans-Pritchard—has essentially been one of metaphysical and epistemological relativism. When working with a group of people, the anthropologist assumes the views of the people they are working with—and, therefore assumes their beliefs in religion, magic, and the efficacy of corresponding rituals are true, usually without ever bothering to explain to the reader how such metaphysical and epistemological views could be true—particularly if the reader holds metaphysical and epistemological views which are ostensibly incompatible (e.g., scientific materialism). The utilization of sensoriums in phenomenological anthropology has the fascinating quality of moving the field beyond its assumptions concerning the truths of what various indigenous people believe—this application of sensoriums actually attempts to show how what such people believe could be true. True in the sense that their beliefs cohere within their worldview, but true also in the sense that objects of their beliefs are empirically experienced by them through their sensoriums. This being said, however, when excerpts of accounts of such phenomena are presented in this book from the ethnography, this we in no way seeks to evaluate the truth or falsity of the accounts presented. Such a venture is both beyond the scope of this book and, more importantly, it is not our purpose for presenting such accounts. Instead, the purpose of examining the accounts is to show that there is an attempt within the accounts to demonstrate that such aforementioned phenomena are empirically real through the utilization of sensoriums. After such attempts have been acknowledged, it is our aim to show that the demonstration adds credence to the indistinguishability of the arbitrary and non-arbitrary nature of things—particularly because the skeptical discoveries can be applied to the phenomena being shown to be empirically real.

Our interest in the placebo effect is less straightforward, though it will involve the understanding that an arbitrary substance—it would seem—is able to render non-arbitrary results with respect to the health and wellness of individuals, to a significant degree. This notion of the "significant degree" of effect, which a placebo is said to possess, is something of a paradox itself. Ever since the Food and Drug Administration (FDA) required the use of placebo test trials to measure the effectiveness of new drugs, the effects of placebos are understood to be the epitome of insignificance, even when they provide tantamount results to the non-arbitrary substances which are competing against them. In this chapter we will explore the idea that the concept of the placebo effect is still quite unclear. Put another way, we will explore the validity of the idea that we do not know what the placebo effect is. We will also explore what has recently been referred to as the "nocebo effect," which is essentially a phenomenon as equally nebulous as the placebo effect, except for the important contrast being that whereas the placebo effect is reported to bring about inexplicable ("inexplicable" here refers to the inability of the current medical materialistic model to provide sufficient explanation concerning why the placebo/nocebo effect works) health and wellness in individuals, the nocebo effect causes inexplicable sickness or disease. We also explore two related phenomena: (1) the phenomenon that patients will ask for placebos because they are aware of the effectiveness of placebos, and even in such situations placebos continue to have effect; and (2) the phenomenon that the placebo effect is getting stronger.

Lastly, when exploring the cogency of the thesis that there is an indistinguishability between the arbitrary and non-arbitrary nature of things, and evaluating whether the placebo effect adds credence to the thesis, we will be interested in the following questions: If we assume for a moment that the natures of things are arbitrary, how does this assumption change our understanding of the placebo effect? Does the placebo effect even make sense, or would such a concept as the "placebo effect" have ever entered into the minds of individuals who believed that the nature of things is actually arbitrary? Along with this line of questioning, we explore the phenomenon of medical professionals, who, rather than attempting to treat an illness with medicine, instead attempt to either utilize or enhance the placebo effect as a preferred form of treatment. This is particularly noteworthy when the medical professional believes that the illness or affliction that the individual is suffering from has been caused by the nocebo effect. In Hegel's topsy-turvy world, can we imagine that the placebo effect is in fact medicine, whereas the nocebo effect is in fact illness?

An Account of Sensoriums Utilized in Phenomenological Anthropology

In the field of phenomenological anthropology, the ethnography that most thoroughly and most abundantly utilizes the concept of sensoriums to attempt to aid the reader in grasping the phenomena being described (to the best of my knowledge) is *Culture and the Senses: Bodily Ways of Knowing in an African Community*, by Kathryn Linn Geurts. Prior to introducing her audience to the particular examples in which she utilizes sensoriums to help her reader grasp the reality of the phenomena being described, Geurts begins, rather by questioning the contemporary, commonsense view of the senses, which she assumes her audience holds uncritically. This uncritical view, Geurts refers to as both a "folk model," as well as a "folk ideology." Concerning these descriptions of this commonsense model of the senses,

Geurts describes at least three crucial characteristics that she wishes her readers to question. After she demonstrates the questionable characteristics of this commonsense model of the senses, as well as presents the data in her ethnography, Geurts puts the idea of sensoriums forward as a critical and more comprehensive alternative theory of the senses.

Geurts finds that the salient features of the folk model of the senses are also its inadequacies. The first salient feature of this model is the belief that humans have five senses (sight, hearing, smell, taste, and touch) and that we passively receive sense data from objects via our senses. Secondly, this folk model also assumes that sense data from one sense does not influence sense data from the other senses. Thirdly, this folk model assumes that the senses are precultural, i.e., it assumes that the culture an individual is a part of does not shape their sensory experiences—but rather individuals across time and space, by and large, have the same sensory experiences—and therefore a type of universality is assumed with respect to human sensory experience. Geurts argues that all three aforementioned characteristics of the folk model are simply not true, and she utilizes the idea of sensoriums to provide a more thorough alternative of understanding empirical experiences.

Geurts challenges the first two salient characteristics of the folk model of the senses by presenting evidence that we have more than five senses, and that the senses influence each other when gathering data, such that there is a sensory order or prioritizing when such senses interact when gathering data. Geurts presents a few distinct, but complementary definitions of what a sensorium is, and one such definition involves this sensory order and integration, in which our senses influence each other. Geurts explains,

> As for the *sensorium*, by that I mean the entire or whole sensory apparatus of the body. In a technical sense, I am using the term the way Laughlin, McManus, and D'Aquili define it in their book *Brain, Symbol, and Experience*: "The *sensorium* is the functional space within the nervous system wherein the phenomenal aspects of the cognized environment are constituted and portrayed in moment-by-moment experience. The sensorium, a time-honored term in science and medicine (Newton used the term in the eighteenth century!), usually refers to the 'whole sensory apparatus of the body' (*Dorland's Illustrated Medical Dictionary*, 23rd ed.). *Phenomenal experience* is a construction mediated by the moment-by-moment reentrainment of perceptual and associative structures. . . . Phenomenal reality is thus in part an entrainment of cognitive and sensorial networks, which is designed to portray

an unfolding world of experience to the organism. The functional space within which association and perception are combined into unitary phenomenal experience is the sensorium" (Laughlin, McManus, and D'Aquili 1992: 106).[1]

Geurts also disagrees with the third salient feature of the folk model of the senses: That the sensory experiences of human beings are universal. Concerning this disagreement, Geurts concedes that she is in the minority opinion in the field of anthropology with respect to this issue, but she cites figures such as Boas, Whorf, and more recently Hallowell, Csordas, Berlin, and Kay[2] who investigate, contribute to, and at times support this

---

1. Geurts, *Culture and the Senses*, 253.

2. Geurts explains some of the developments from Boas's initial assertion that perception is not precultural to contemporary finding which lend support for such a claim. Geurts writes, "For example, at the turn of the century interest in optical illusions led to a series of test by British psychologist and ethnologist W. H. R. Rivers that led to the 'carpentered-world hypothesis' (Bock 1988: 10–11). Simply put, this proposal suggests that people who grow up in an environment that is highly carpentered will learn to use angles in perceiving distance whereas those who live in round or oval houses will not develop such perceptual habits. And while additional research has been carried out on the susceptibility to illusion of differing populations (Segal, Campbell, and Herskovits 1966), the conclusions drawn are merely that the basic process of perception is the same for all human groups and that where differences occur it is due to experience rather than a result of inherent 'racial' or 'biological' distinction. Questions about the influence of language on perception were taken up by Edward Sapir and Benjamin Lee Whorf, who concluded that the effects were probably more on conceptual structure than at the actual level of perception (Whorf 1956: 158). Hallowell (1951, 1955) was concerned with how cultural structuring of perception influenced personality organization and the practical experiences of the individual, but his ideas were not followed up until quite recently (Csordas 1994b). Other significant contributions to the study of culture and perception include work on proxemics and the ethnography of communication, which clearly demonstrated cultural variation in attention to and use of different sense modalities (E. T. Hall 1959, 1966). At the other end of the spectrum is ethnosemantic research, which suggested that color terminology 'evolves' in societies from a simple to complex set in a fairly uniform order—implying a universality to the way human groups apprehend certain 'basic' colors (Berlin and Kay 1969). However, controversy over this and subsequent color terminology research continues (see Block 1988: 173–175 and more significantly, Lucy 1992: 177–187 for a thorough review and critique, especially in relation to the question of linguistic relativity), the details of which are somewhat beyond the scope of this study. Two things stand out about this small body of literature. First, most of the work—from Boas to Berlin and Kay—focuses primarily on sight or on audiovisual perception, neglecting other bodily and sensory modes such as touching, tasting, and olfaction (although Hall's work is an exception). Second, while there is good evidence that perception is culturally shaped, it is a research arena that has been neglected by anthropology." Geurts, *Culture and the Senses*, 11–12.

point of view—but she also wishes for the reader to know that despite such contributions this area in anthropology suffers from neglect. To this point Geurts explains,

> My study has as one of its precedents a long-standing though minority or even marginalized interest within anthropology in issues of perception. These concerns date back as far as 1883, when Boas's Baffinland study of how Eskimos perceived the color of seawater led him to conclude that the eye was "not a mere physical organ but a means of perception conditioned by the tradition in which its possessor has been reared" (Ruth Benedict quoted in Stocking 1968: 145). Subsequent studies have either agreed with Boas or concluded that the most salient aspects of human perception are precultural, and research has not advanced much beyond these two basic claims.[3]

Given the evidence that Geurts presents concerning sensory experience not being a precultural given, she then argues for the idea that culture has an active influence is shaping the sensoriums of people, and by implication, that cultural difference can then lead to differences in sensoriums. Quoting from Walter Ong's *Presence of the Word* to illustrate how a sensorium may provide unique and varied sensory experiences, Geurts includes the following explanation concerning sensoriums; she notes that

> "it is useful to think of cultures in terms of the organization of the sensorium. By the sensorium we mean here the entire sensory apparatus as an operational complex.... [D]ifferences in cultures... can be thought of as differences in the sensorium, the organization of which is in part determined by culture while at the same time it makes culture.... Man's sensory perceptions are abundant and overwhelming. He cannot attend to them all at once. In great part a given culture teaches him one or another way of productive specialization. It brings him to organize his sensorium by attending to some types of perception more than others, by making an issue of certain ones while relatively neglecting other ones" (originally from Ong's book *The Presence of the Word*, but more recently reprinted in David Howes's *Varieties of Sensory Experience* [1991: 28].[4]

Geurts further grounds her perspective philosophically, relying on the ideas of Bourdieu's *habitus* and Merleau-Ponty's idea of *preobjective*. Such ideas by Merleau-Ponty and Bourdieu, prior to Geurts, have already been

---

3. Geurts, *Culture and the Senses*, 11.
4. Geurts, *Culture and the Senses*, 253.

utilized by Csordas in the field of phenomenological anthropology—but as we will soon observe, Geurts's application of these ideas is much more profound. Expressing her reliance on Merleau-Ponty, Geurts explains, "the assertion that perception begins in the body and ends in objects (rather than the other way around) has been borrowed from Merleau-Ponty and applied to anthropological issues so that we can address the question of cultural mediation in apprehension of one's environment and apprehension of one's own orientational states (Csordas 1990: 9), or what Hallowell called (1955) the 'behavioral environment of the self.'"[5]

Concerning the idea of Bourdieu's habitus, we find the philosophical framework necessary to imagine how a sensorium is shaped by culture. This is evident particularly with the phrase which Geurts frequently utilizes, i.e., "the process by which history is turned into nature."[6] Incorporating these philosophical ideas into the structure of her ethnography (so that the reader may better understand the phenomena presented) allows Geurts to express the following sentiment,

> to my theoretical point of view, I believe that in a cultural community's sensorium[7] we find refracted some of the values that they hold so dear that they literally make these themes or these motifs into "body." In other words, a cultural community's sensory order reflects aspects of the world that are so precious to the members of that community that (although they remain largely

---

5. Geurts, *Culture and the Senses*, 15.
6. Geurts, *Culture and the Senses*, 10.
7. Note the phrase "cultural community's sensorium"; this definitely suggests that there can be different tokens of the same type of sensoriums enabling communities to share sensory experiences while at the same time allowing for different sensory experiences to likewise be shared by a different community with a different cultural community sensorium. An interesting question becomes: To what extent can we frame such a situation within the context of Hegel's topsy-turvy world thought-experiment? Two considerations must be made for such a framework to begin to be superimposed over the situation. First, we have to remove the idea that one world is phenomenal while the other is Noumenal and we must merely suppose that there are two worlds, both phenomenal in nature. Second, we may have to concede that the extreme which Hegel proposes—i.e., that the worlds are the complete inversion of each other, may not necessarily be the case. After we make these two considerations, however, the insight from Hegel's topsy-turvy world thought experiment, appears to describe this situation quite well: We observe that there are two worlds, and in each of these worlds all the individuals appear to have the same phenomenal experiences—with respect to each world the experiences are universal and appear non-arbitrary. When, however, the two worlds encounter each other and their two sets of "universal" experiences differ, will each world think the other world's experiences to be incorrect and ultimately arbitrary?

unconscious and habitual) they are the things that children growing up in this culture developmentally come to carry in their very bodies. So the senses, I believe, are ways of embodying cultural categories, or making into body certain values or aspects of *being* that the particular cultural community has historically deemed precious and dear.[8]

With this interpretive philosophical framework in mind, Geurts presents the most radical aspect of her ethnography. Let us present this aspect in the form of a question: What if a people in a particular milieu decided to hone a particular sense—a sense that Geurts explains we do not even include in our folk model of the senses, but nevertheless an empirical sense—how different would not only their phenomenological experience be from ours, but also, how different would their empirical experience be? Geurts's ethnography presents such radically different, yet no less empirically real experiences of such a group of people she worked with.

The particular community Geurts is working with are Anlo-Ewe speaking people who live in the Volta Region in southeastern Ghana. The sense that plays a primary role in the ordering of their cultural community's sensorium is the sense of balance. Concerning how the sense of balance is honed Geurts explains that "relatively speaking, Anlo-Ewe people seem to give it [balance] a discursive and practical priority that Euro-Americans do not. Most Anlo-Ewe people grow up being encouraged to actively balance; they learn to balance their own bodies as infants, they balance small bowls and pans on their heads as toddlers, they carry books and desks on their heads when walking to and from school, and they grow into an adult orientation in which balance is considered a defining characteristic of mature persons and the human species in general (hence an important dimension of their ethos)."[9] Another important sense described as an integral part of this community's sensorium is a feeling in the skin referred to as seselelame. In the glossary of her ethnography Geurts defines seselelame as "hearing or feeling in the body, flesh, or skin; a cultural category for sensation, emotion, disposition, and vocation."[10] After describing these senses, Geurts explains that it is her understanding that these two senses, along with what we commonly refer to as the five senses of the folk model of the sense, are integrated in such a way in this cultural community's sensorium

8. Geurts, *Culture and the Senses*, 10.
9. Geurts, *Culture and the Senses*, 5.
10. Geurts, *Culture and the Senses*, 283.

that the Anlo-Ewe speaking people of this community are able to have empirically real experiences (i.e., sensory experiences) that correspond to their religious and philosophical practices of vodu—as well as the gods associated with phenomena of nature.

In a moment we will examine one such account, which Geurts details in her ethnography, but before we do so, let us examine how she explains such an account ontologically and epistemologically (i.e., experientially). After describing an account involving an individual referred to as "Janice" who experiences affliction due to Vodu, Geurts explains,

> This story illustrates a continuity between the experiential and the ontological. For Janice, *vodu* had an unconscious though clear link to her sense of well-being, even though she had strived (in a more or less cognitive or intellectual way) to disavow it, in part because of her adherence to Christianity. The metaphysics summed up in this experience involving *vodu* is not a superficial idea that can be easily discarded, nor is it a religious cult that can be joined. Rather, *vodu* is a deeply embodied phenomenon residing largely in the domain of *seselelame* while being pervasive in Anlo cultural logic: an idea reminiscent of Bourdieu's habitus (1977: 78–95) as "history turned into nature."[11]

Let us now examine that account, and afterward, we will analyze it with respect to the three skeptical discoveries, and the overall thesis that there persists an indistinguishability between the arbitrary and the nonarbitrary nature of things. Here is the account:

> Janice grew up in the Volta Region of Ghana, in and around what was deemed the Anlo homeland, but as an adult she spent about twelve years in Britain training as a nurse-midwife. She then returned to her hometown in the Volta Region and built a "maternity home," or what we might call a "women's health clinic." When I [Geurts] worked with her she was an active and high-level member of the professional organization known as the Ghana Registered Midwives Association, and she continued to travel abroad to conferences and for pleasure. While Janice professed mostly scorn and disbelief in *vodu* and related phenomena, she took me to meet a priest of a *vodu* center near her clinic and home. She felt that as a student of Anlo-Ewe culture I needed to be exposed to all facets of life, but she did not conceal her belief that this man was ignorant, superstitious, and backward. She also knew that he was opposed

---

11. Geurts, *Culture and the Senses*, 195.

to her efforts to bring "development" and health-care services to this area. In serving together on a local district council, she felt that he blocked her efforts to educate and improve the quality of life of young women and was against her efforts to disburse information about family planning, contraception, and AIDS. She felt his attitudes were directly related to his "traditional religious beliefs," which included the relegation of women to childbearing and domestic services. Accordingly, I was received by this *vodu* priest in a less than warm and cordial way, and the meeting was quite brief and uneventful. However, as we left the center, Janice recounted the following story.

When she returned from Britain in the early 1970s, Janice had cause to interact (on a number of occasions) with various members of this *vodu* center. At the end of one particular meeting they suggested she bring a goat to sacrifice at the shrine. Holding strongly negative beliefs about such "sacrificial rituals," Janice went home and forgot the request. A week later she became ill, visited the (hospital) doctor, took several courses of medicine, but failed to improve. Janice explained that she felt not only fatigue but also "hounded by something" as if it were "hovering" about her or "following" her around.

One day shortly thereafter Janice ran into an acquaintance who had studied the art of "spiritual healing." Without her reporting anything to him about her illness, the man suggested to Janice that something was following her. He expressed intense concern, explaining that it was invisible so he did not expect she could see it but wondered whether she had been experiencing some kind of "shadow effect." He asked if she had made a promise and failed to fulfill it. Despite her surprise at his acute perception of her sensations, Janice remembered no promise and the sickness endured. Weeks later she suddenly recalled the demand for a goat made by members of the *vodu* shrine, and she realized this "coerced promise" fit her healer friend's notion of the etiology of her illness. She promptly delivered a goat to the *vodu* priest, and after months of having felt desperately ill, Janice reported that she recovered within two or three days.[12]

In this account, we are presented with what Geurts refers to as "a continuity between the experiential and the ontological." It is this continuity which we want to suggest adds credence to the indistinguishability between arbitrary and non-arbitrary nature with respect to things. It is also the

12. Geurts, *Culture and the Senses*, 194–95.

concept of a sensorium which allows Geurts to present the reality of this continuity. In this account we have an individual referred to as "Janice," who grew up in a particular milieu, which shaped her particular culture community's sensorium—one in which she shares with other Anlo-Ewe speaking people of that particular milieu. This particular culture community's sensorium, which is a part of her, was formed and informed by a particular history and particular corresponding cultural practices that Janice experienced in this particular milieu. According to Geurts's explanation, her sensorium is the embodiment of the values of these cultural practices present and preserved in history. Such a process is evidence for Geurts of Bourdieu's idea of habitus, and it is an example of "history turned into nature." It is also important to note that although Janice's philosophical and theological beliefs changed away from *vodu* and to Christianity, (Geurts appears to suggest that) Janice cannot change the structure of her sensorium in the same manner as she can change the structure and content of her philosophical and theological beliefs.

It would appear in this account that Janice, the *vodu* priest, and the individual familiar with "spiritual healing" each have sensoriums similar in type, or that they share a cultural community's sensorium (though it is somewhat unclear from the account if the *vodu* priest shares the same sensorium—one makes this assumption if one supposes he did something negative to cause Janice to become ill—but this conclusion is not specified in the account it is only implicit). In this cultural community's sensorium it is the sense of *seselelame* where the effects of *vodu* are felt—Geurts explains as much when she states, "*vodu* is a deeply embodied phenomenon residing largely in the domain of *seselelame* while being pervasive in Anlo cultural logic."[13] Because of the particular sensorium that Janice has, she is effected by the negative effects of *vodu*—by what is vaguely described in the account as being "'hounded by something,' as if it were 'hovering' about her or 'following' her around," and as a "shadow effect." If Geurts explanation of the account is metaphysically accurate, then we are left to concluded that both Janice and the individual familiar with "spiritual healing," both empirically experienced this phenomenon—i.e., that this "shadow effect" is an empirically real phenomenon that can be experienced through the particular sense of *seselelame*. We now see what is meant by a continuity between the experiential and the ontological—but we also see

---

13. Geurts, *Culture and the Senses*, 195.

that this continuity makes it difficult to distinguish between the arbitrary and the non-arbitrary nature of things.

Let us now observe what occurs if we attempt to question whether the nature of this "shadow effect"—this something which follows, hovers, and hounds—is arbitrary or non-arbitrary. The justification we encounter is disturbingly circular. Through Geurts's explanation of the account, we grasp that the experience of this "thing in question," is empirical in nature. We also grasp that this "thing in question" is empirical in the particular way that it is because a particular history has been turned into a particular embodied nature—an embodied nature that is able to experience the nature of this "thing in question." Had a different history been embodied, or the same history been embodied differently, then perhaps a different nature of the "thing in question" would be empirically experienced—or perhaps the "thing in question" would not be experienced at all. If the experience of a thing is contingent on the embodied history of the subject (i.e., the embodied history of a community of subjects)—which Geurts's ideas concerning sensoriums explains that it must be—then how are we able to distinguish between the arbitrary and the non-arbitrary nature of things?

If we examine this situation with respect to the first skeptical discovery, we find some striking similarities to the account which Geurts's has provided and which uses the concept of sensoriums in the overall explanation of the events in the account. The first skeptical discovery was derived from the situation Hegel presents to his readers which involves the topsy-turvy world thought-experiment. Given the epistemological situation of a division between the noumenal and the phenomenal world, Hegel is able to suggest that our phenomenological experiences could in fact be the exact opposite of what the object's nature truly is in the noumenal world. The phenomenal nature we experience empirically would be arbitrary in this situation; whereas the nature of the object as it is in itself in the noumenal world would be non-arbitrary. The first skeptical discovery explains that what is universal can be compatible with what is arbitrary. This discovery implicitly provides an epistemological caution that if something's nature appears to be universal then it may still be arbitrary.

The interesting (or perhaps not so interesting but rather incomplete) thing about the topsy-turvy world thought-experiment is that it never provides any explanation as to how the phenomenal world could be topsy-turvy. This thought-experiment simply alerts us to the epistemological possibility that the phenomenal world and everything in it could be the inverse of the noumenal world. Geurts's portrayal of sensoriums, on the other hand, helps to supply us with both a conceptual framework (utilizing the ideas of Merleau-Ponty and Bourdieu) as well as particular examples of variations in sensory experience, to help us to grasp how the universal empirical experience of phenomena within the context of a particular world or culture community's sensorium is possible; Geurts's portrayal of sensoriums also aids us in grasping how a variety of empirical experiences exist between varying cultural community's sensoriums and how the empirical experience of one cultural community's sensorium could be the inverse of another cultural community's sensorium. This portrayal and utilization of sensoriums, we argue, adds credence to the idea that there exists an indistinguishability between the arbitrary and the non-arbitrary nature of things, in presenting a situation that is epistemologically similar to that of the topsy-turvy world. In addition, it offers no discernment concerning whether the nature of such empirical experiences—experiences that are drastically different from one cultural community's sensorium to the next—are arbitrary or non-arbitrary. The use of sensoriums in phenomenological anthropology provides us with a framework which allows us to make a comparison between our own epistemological situation and that of the topsy-turvy world thought experiment in which we can have no certainty as to whether the objects we experience have arbitrary or non-arbitrary natures. This ethnography utilized sensoriums to demonstrate how there can exist universal empirical experience within a particular milieu (via a culture community's sensorium) as well as how variations among worlds (via different histories becoming embodied in communities' sensoriums) such that various particular sensoriums are different and are therefore able to have different empirical experiences.

We also observe aspects of the second skeptical discovery in the account of "Janice" that is described in Geurts's ethnography. This is the discovery that coherence epistemologies make it difficult, or perhaps impossible to know whether the claims of one's coherent system bear any correspondence to actuality. Given this discovery—and particularly when taken in conjunction with the first skeptical discovery—an epistemological worry becomes that coherence epistemologies have the potential to manifest and facilitate the inverse of what actually, in fact, is (Recall this suggestion which Verene puts forth concerning phrenology being the inverse of phenomenology). In this account we do observe a form of coherence in the phenomena involving *vodu*—a coherence that Janice is involved in, but one, which we as the reader remain uncertain as to whether she ascribes any truth to. This coherence involves what appears to be a cause and effect relationship between Janice failing to keep a "promise" to sacrifice a goat, and her sudden decline in health; as well as her sudden recovery upon fulfilling this promise. Given Janice's rejection of *vodu*, the coherence which relates these aforementioned events initially appears absent from her worldview. For example, she does not immediately say upon falling ill: "Oh, this illness must be due to that goat I forgot to sacrifice." Rather she "visited the (hospital) doctor" and "took several courses and medicine, but failed to improve."

It is further explained that it is not until Janice sacrifices the goat that her health improves. This action of sacrificing the goat—if looked at in the context of Janice's belief system, which is a belief in the efficacy of contemporary medicine and a disbelief in the efficacy of the practices of *vodu*—should have no effect on her health. We can observe how a particular coherent system of beliefs can provide a form of reasoning in which one remains uncertain as to whether such reasoning bears any resemblance to actuality—which is the worry of the second skeptical discovery. We perceive the uncertainty which this account aims to render when we ask specific questions of the account such as: Is the relationship between Janice sacrificing a goat and Janice's health improving arbitrary or non-arbitrary? In the same manner we can ask whether the relationship between Janice not keeping her promise and Janice becoming ill is arbitrary or non-arbitrary. The true nature of the relationships between events appears difficult to distinguish given the competing frameworks for knowledge. From within the coherent system of reason which *vodu* provides, these events appear non-arbitrary and can be understood as having a cause-and-effect relationship. When viewed from outside the coherent system of *vodu*, for example, from within the contemporary approaches to medicine that Janice received in Britain, the cause and effect claims of *vodu* are understood to be arbitrary, superstitious associations with no substantial cause and effect relations to each other. This example is quite interesting because of the contrast it shows. Janice's cultural community's sensorium embodies the "cultural logic" of *vodu*, according to Geurts—yet as Geurts explains, Janice had disavowed the beliefs of *vodu* cognitively. One can imagine aspects of this account, phenomenologically speaking, to contain aspect which would seem counterintuitive at the very least, and perhaps even topsy-turvy—e.g., actions that appear neutral with respect to health in one world are actually unhealthy in another world (i.e., not keeping ones promise) and actions that also appear neutral in relation to health in one world are actually healthy actions in another world (i.e., sacrificing a goat to keep a promise); likewise actions that are seen as health in this other world (going to a hospital when ill and receiving treatment) are seen as neutral in the former world.

The next account involves the phenomenal experience of the god Nyigbla, who—according to the Anlo-Ewe speaking people Geurts worked with—is associated with lightning (among other things). These Anlo-speaking people Geurts worked with explain that they perceive the god Nyigbla during some but not all phenomena of lightning. This admission by such individuals causes Geurts to seek clarification concerning how these individuals are able to distinguish between Nyigbla in the form of lightning and (what is referred to in the ethnography as) "common lightning." Toward the end of these accounts Geurts does not provide a thorough answer to this question per se, but rather provides an interesting and complex analogy comparing the Anlo-speaking people's ability to discern between Nyigbla and "common lightning," and the assumed reader's ability to distinguish fact from fiction on television. Geurts concludes the account and questions in the account concerning the nature of "common lightning" being different from the experience of Nyigbla in the form of lightning, by again referring to the sensorium, and in particular to the sense of seselelame, explaining, "These are questions that can be more fully addressed through attention to the sensorium. Metaphysical forces within Anlo worlds were perceived and known largely through the sensory fields, with particular attention to a synesthetic ability they valued in *seselelame*."[14]

Let us now examine this account:

> The fear of being struck by lightning and the symbolic magnitude of such an event was great. As another *mɔfiala*[15] explained: "People are afraid that when they go to steal, *thunder will come into the family* and people will be disgraced." An individual's death by lightning (referred to by some as *tohonɔfui*) was a reflection on all his kin since it signified a transgression of such import that Nyigbla involved himself. This phenomenon illustrates the intricate connections among self, society, and cosmos; when a person heard the crash of thunder or witnessed the night sky light up like day, the shudder that reverberated through his body was not simply a "personal" experience of fear, but rather that shudder

---

14. Geurts, *Culture and the Senses*, 181.

15. Geurts defines this word as "one who leads or shows the road, leader, teacher, guide; forefinger, index." Geurts, *Culture and the Senses*, 283.

embodied the sticky web of relations linking individual, social, and cosmic fields of being (cf. Jackson and Karp 1990) Lack of attention paid to *agabagbadodo* (balancing) created disruptions in these links (largely through violations of moral laws) and resulted in serious illnesses and general *xexeme gbegble* (ruin or destruction of the world).

In addition, one *mɔfiala* explained to me that as he sat in his family house at Anloga, he experienced Nyigbla flying above the lagoon from Anyako to Alakple. This young man described the experience as beginning with a tremendous rumbling, like the galloping sound of horses running in the distance. Next appeared a white light in the sky, which gradually took the shape of a horse mounted by a human being. I asked him to explain the difference between thunder and lightning in relation to this manifestation of Nyigbla. His response focused on the feeling he had (*seselelame*) and how his family knew it was Nyigbla because of the semi-paralysis that set into his body immediately after this experience. The paralysis and stupefaction disappeared only after various purification rites were performed. This situation did not simply present an impending storm with dramatic thunder and lightning. Nyigbla's presence was known through the feeling in the young man's body or his compromised state of health.

An Anlo-speaking person's perception of the distinction between Nyigbla and common lightning could be compared to the difference in our culture between turning on the television to a fictionalized movie as opposed to turning on the television to a newscast announcing a tornado touching down a half mile from our house. How do we know the difference? Is it only through what we can see? What is the nature of the aesthetic difference in our perception and ability to distinguish? These are questions that can be more fully addressed through attention to the sensorium. Metaphysical forces within Anlo worlds were perceived and known largely through the sensory fields, with particular attention to a synesthetic ability they valued in *seselelame*.[16]

In this account we observe a similar type of phenomena as in the former account. We read of an empirical experience of a divine being through the sense or "synesthetic ability" of *seselelame*. This experience is taken to be empirically real given that it is of the senses. At the same time this empirical experience appears contingent on the particular history and practices which are embodied in a particular cultural community's sensorium,

---

16. Geurts, *Culture and the Senses*, 180–81.

which allows for the possibility of such an empirical experience. The second skeptical discovery articulates the worry that one's system of reasoning, although internally coherent, may not bear any resemblance to actuality. We observe elements of the worry of this skeptical discovery in this account in much the same manner as we did with the former account. Take, for example, the event of the *mɔfiala*'s compromised health after witnessing the presence of Nyigbla in the lightning. Is there any actual cause and effect relationship between these two events? In a similar manner we can inquire concerning the *mɔfiala*'s health returning to him after the "various purification rites" performed.

With this account, however, let us also examine the third skeptical discovery in a more general form. The third skeptical discovery asks the question concerning whether the form of self-consciousness that Hegel provides to the reader corresponds to the divine mind, or rather if it is merely a product of his own creativity. If we generalize this third skeptical discovery we arrive at a concern quite similar to the former one pertaining to the second skeptical discovery. This concerning being: If the history that a particular culture embodies—a history that describes particular deities as actually existing—allows such deities to be experienced by a culture community's sensorium, then how do we know that such individuals are actually experiencing such deities, as opposed to merely experiencing their particular history embodied in their sensoriums? A further, and equally perplexing question is whether it makes sense to draw a distinction between these two options—perhaps these two options are merely different sides of the same coin so to speak. We do not aim to answer such a question, but rather, only to show that the difficulties—epistemologically speaking—such questions bring add greater cogency to the position of epistemological agnosticism concerning the indistinguishability between the arbitrary and non-arbitrary nature of things.

Describing Placebos/Nocebos and Their Effect

In this section we will look at the most comprehensive ways in which placebos/nocebos and the placebo effect/nocebo effect has been defined as well as examine to what extent if any the placebo effect is understood. We will then examine the implications of placebos in the context of placebo test trials given our lack of understanding concerning what placebos are and of how they work. This is done in relation to the position of epistemological agnosticism in relation to the indistinguishability of arbitrary and non-arbitrary nature. We put forth the idea for consideration that if an arbitrary substance provides tantamount effects to that of a non-arbitrary substance, then such results add credence to our position; whereas when non-arbitrary substances outperform placebos, then such agnosticism should ostensibly be met with greater skepticism.

Perhaps the most comprehensive work which has been writing on placebos and their effects is *The Power Placebo* by Arthur K. Shapiro and Elaine Shapiro. In this work they propose the following definition of both a placebo and the placebo effect. With this definition they aim for thoroughness while avoiding tautology. They explain that "a placebo is any therapy (or that component of any therapy) that is intentionally or knowingly used for its nonspecific, psychological, or psychophysiological, therapeutic effect, or that is used for a presumed specific therapeutic effect on a patient, symptom, or illness but is without specific activity[17] for the condition being treated. A placebo, when used as a control in experimental studies, is a substance or procedure that is without specific activity for the condition being treated. The placebo effect is the nonspecific psychological or psychophysiological therapeutic effect produced by a placebo."[18] The aspect of this definition which allows for a rather expansive understanding of the placebo effect is explained with the phrase "or that is used for a presumed specific therapeutic effect on a patient, symptom, or illness but is without specific activity." This allows treatments which were believed to have therapeutic effect, but which in fact do not to be included as placebos. Shapiro and Shapiro enumerate the following phenomena as treatments which they understanding to be placebos, stating,

> The treatment, however, is not limited to drugs. It can take the form not only of oral, parenteral, and topical drugs but also of magic; religious rituals (such as prayer and exorcism); incantations; intubation or incubation; purgation (in the form of clysterization, phlebotomy, catharsis, vomachics, diaphoretics, and other forms of dehydrations or reductions of guilt by ridding the body of the bad or evil); and cleansing the mind by talking out the evil (as in psychoanalysis and psychotherapy). The medium for these

---

17. Shapiro and Shapiro utilize the phrase "without specific activity" as an alternative to such descriptions as "inert" or "inactive" because they explain that "even substances such as distilled water and lactose can cause bodily changes," which can be seen as activity. Shapiro and Shapiro, *The Powerful Placebo*, 35.

18. Shapiro and Shapiro, *The Powerful Placebo*, 41.

myriad treatments, of course, is the placebo, and the underlying matrix for its effectiveness is the powerful placebo effect.[19]

With the efficacy of the many and various treatments throughout prescientific medical history falling under the label of placebo effect, it causes Shapiro and Shapiro to put forth the startling claim "that history [the prescientific medical history] provides ample evidence for the hypothesis that until recently the history of medical treatment was essentially the history of the placebo effect."[20] This hypothesis provides us with an outlook on prescientific medical history which suggest an indistinguishability between the arbitrary and the non-arbitrary nature of things/treatments.[21] Put another way, although an individual may continue to provide a treatment, which the individual earnestly believes to possess healing properties, and although individuals who receive this treatment experience the healing that was professed to be the result of the treatment—it is in fact the case that the treatment has an arbitrary relationship to the healing experienced by individuals after receiving the treatment. The arbitrary nature of such a relationship, however, appears indistinguishable from that of what would be understood as the non-arbitrary nature of the relationship. This indistinguishability between the arbitrary nature of medical treatment and the non-arbitrary nature of medical treatment in prescientific medical history should ostensibly change with the advent of science, and in particular with the advent of placebo test trials. We will now proceed to examine this change, as well as to examine how the nocebo effect may complicate the objective evaluation which is characteristic of this change.

The earliest placebo test trials or double-blind test occurred as early as 1908 with laboratory test to determine the effects of alcohol and other drugs on fatigue—this test was conducted by W. H. R. Rivers. The

---

19. Shapiro and Shapiro, *The Powerful Placebo*, 1.
20. Shapiro and Shapiro, *The Powerful Placebo*, 2.
21. The language used by Shapiro and Shapiro when discussing placebos and the placebo effect does not utilize phrases such as "arbitrary nature of a thing" or "non-arbitrary nature of a thing"; instead the phrase "specific activity" and "without specific activity" are used. One can however substitute the latter terminology for the former and still retain the meaning of the former because what is being suggested by the former terminology is that there is a specific activity or effect which the nature of a substance is supposed to possess or bring about, and when such an activity or effect is produced, but it is later found that the activity or effect was not caused by the substance, then it can be expressed that the relationship of the activity to the nature of the substance is arbitrary, or that it is "without specific activity."

double-blind aspect of the trial refers to the condition in which neither the patient nor the doctor have knowledge of whether the drug being provided to the patient is, either a placebo, or whether it is a substance with the property to produce a specific activity which would produce the intended effect of the treatment. The effectiveness of the treatment is measured against the effectiveness of the placebo, in which the treatment's effectiveness must outperform the placebo effect in order for it to be considered effective. The placebo test trials help to rule out a variety of factors which may contribute to the placebo effect including, both the expectation of patients and physicians concerning the effectiveness of the treatment, as well as physicians or patients' enthusiasm toward the treatment. By removing such bias in the test trials a measure of objective evaluation is aimed at, with the rationale being that once such bias is removed in the double-blind test, then if the substance or treatment being tested outperforms the placebo, one can say with certainty that the effect of the treatment is more than merely the placebo effect. One is able to conclude that the substance or treatment contains the property to produce a specific activity which is the intended result of the treatment. It is this situation which distinguishes scientific medicine from prescientific medicine—this situation of the placebo test trial allows one to ostensibly distinguish between the arbitrary and non-arbitrary nature of treatments.

We would tend to share this sentiment concerning the objective evaluation involved in scientific medicine, but we find that the nocebo effect complicates matters in a significant way, one in which makes the arbitrary and non-arbitrary nature of medical treatments more difficult to distinguish. The nocebo effect is defined as

> the causation of sickness (or death) by expectations of sickness (or death) and by associated emotional states. There are two forms of the nocebo effect. In the *specific* form, the subject expects a particular negative outcome and that outcome consequently occurs. For example, a surgical patient expects to die on the operating table and does die—not from the surgery itself, but from the expectation and associated affect. . . . In the *generic* form, subjects have vague negative expectations. For example, they are diffusely pessimistic—and their expectations are realized in terms of symptoms, sickness, or death—none of which were specifically expected.[22]

---

22. Hahn, "The Nocebo Phenomenon," 56–57.

The nocebo effect is also distinct from negative side-effects of the placebo effect; an example of the latter being a rash that may develop on a patient after the patient is given medicine which they are allergic to—however the medicine is not the actual substance which the patient is allergic to, but rather it is a placebo. In this latter example the negative reaction is not to be understood as the nocebo effect—because the patient was not having negative expectations about the treatment—but only anticipated a negative side-effect of a positive treatment. Given the qualities of the nocebo effect, we find it difficult to initially determine which aliments are arbitrary in nature and which aliments are non-arbitrary in nature.

We find that this determination is made prima facie by the metaphysical commitments of the medical/scientific community so that particular phenomena are automatically excluded based on their contrary metaphysical assumptions to that of the paradigm of the medical/scientific community. An example of such a phenomena would be "voodoo death" which was described by physiologist Walter Cannon as "a fatal power of the imagination working through unmitigated terror."[23] When individuals experience the nocebo effect from voodoo, for example, illness from a voodoo hex,[24] and medicines are provided but in no way aid the patient in there recovery, medical professionals may employ appropriate placebo treatments to cure the patient from illnesses brought about by the nocebo effect. In such a situation, we would like to suggest that a topsy-turvy type of scenario occurs. In this situation we have an illness brought about by the nocebo effect, but an illness nonetheless that can have as grave as consequences as any illness not brought about by the nocebo effect. In this situation we observe that the illness brought about by the nocebo effect is unable to be cured by the contemporary medicines available to the physicians, but that a placebo which appropriately relates to the illness is able to provide the patient with a viable treatment or cure to the illness brought about by the nocebo effect. The following topsy-turvy type of situation can be observed in the follow case:

23. Cannon, "Voodoo Death," 170.

24. Here let us define "Voodoo Hex" in a similar manner to the way in which Clifton K. Meador defines "Hex Death" in his article, "Hex Death: Voodoo Magic or Persuasion?" In this article he explains that "Hex Death is a death that follows a ritualized pronouncement of death by someone perceived by the subject to have immense power and authority. When death follows, it is attributed by the local community to the words and actions of the hexing individual." In a similar way we can define "Voodoo Hex" as "[negative results] that follows a ritualized pronouncement of these [negative results] by someone perceived by the subject to have immense power and authority." Meador, "Hex Death," 244.

The patient [who is referred to as Vanders] had been ill for many weeks and had lost a large amount of weight. He looked wasted and near death. Although results of the physical examination and laboratory studies were negative, tuberculosis or widespread cancer was considered the likely diagnosis. The patient refused to eat and continued a downhill course despite a feeding tube, saying repeatedly that he was going to die. He soon reached a stage of near stupor, coming in and out of consciousness, and was barely able to talk. Only then did his wife, who had stayed by his bed, ask to talk to Dr. Daugherty privately.

[It is then explained that Vanders's wife shares with Dr. Daugherty that her husband got into an argument with a voodoo priest who consequently cursed him by waiving a "foul-smelling liquid" in Vander's face and as a result of the curse Vanders would die.]

Dr. Daugherty spent many hours that evening pondering the bewildering story and considering what he could do to save this moribund man. The next morning he gathered 10 or more of the patient's kin at the bedside; they were trembling and frightened to be associated with this doomed man. Dr. Daugherty announced in his most authoritative voice that he now knew exactly what was wrong. He told them of a harrowing encounter at midnight the night before in the local cemetery, where Dr. Daugherty had lured the voodoo priest on some false pretense. Dr. Daugherty said he told the priest that he had uncovered his secret voodoo and found out precisely how he had voodooed Vanders. Dr. Daugherty reported that the priest had laughed at him, but that Dr. Daugherty then choked him against a tree nearly to death until the priest described exactly what he had done. Dr. Daugherty announced to the astonished patient and family, "That voodoo priest made you breathe in some lizard eggs and they climbed down into your stomach and hatched out some small lizards. All but one of them died leaving one large one which is eating up all your food and the lining of your body. I will now get that lizard out of your system and cure you of his horrible curse." With that, he summoned the nurse. She had, on prearrangement, filled a large syringe with apomorphine (a powerful parenteral emetic). With great ceremony Dr. Daugherty pointed the syringe to the ceiling and inspected it most carefully for several moments. He squirted the smallest amount of clear liquid into the air and lunged toward the patient, who by now had gathered enough strength to be sitting up wide-eyed in the bed. Although he pressed himself against the headboard trying to withdraw from the injection, Dr. Daugherty pushed the needle into the patient's arm and delivered the full dose of apomorphine. With that he wheeled about, said nothing, and dramatically left the ward.

Within a few minutes the nurse reported that the patient was beginning to vomit. When Dr. Daugherty arrived at the bedside Vanders was retching, one wave of spasms after another. His head was buried in a metal basin that sat on the bed. After several minutes of continued vomiting and at a point judged to be near its end, Dr. Daugherty pulled from his black bag, artfully and secretively, a live green lizard. At the height of the next wave of retching he slid the lizard into the basin. He called out in a loud voice, "Look what has come out of you! You are now cured. The voodoo curse is lifted. . . . Within a week the patient was discharged home, and soon regained his weight and strength. He lived another 10 or more years, having no further encounter with the voodoo priest, and died of an apparent heart attack. No one else in the family was affected."[25]

We selected this particular case as a template of such a topsy-turvy scenario in particular, because there is a level of deception between the physician and the patient such that we the audience—unlike the patient—know what actually happened (i.e., we know that Vanders does not vomit up a lizard, but rather was fooled into thinking that he did as part of the placebo cure). This feature of the account, we argue, makes the indistinguishability between the arbitrary and non-arbitrary nature between illness and treatment more salient. Let us now examine the topsy-turvy qualities of this account.

We begin by pointing out the claim made by Shapiro and Shapiro that the history of prescientific medicine was, in essence, the history of the placebo effect. In this situation there persisted an indistinguishability between the arbitrary and non-arbitrary nature of the relationship between illnesses and treatments. With the advent of scientific medicine, and with that, the use of placebo test trials, a method for distinguishing arbitrary relationships from non-arbitrary relationships between that of illness and treatment emerges. With this emergence also proceeds the ostensible confidence that there exist non-arbitrary relationships between illnesses and treatments, which can be correctly identified through this scientific process. It is this scientific medical model, we argue, that becomes inverted with the phenomenon of the nocebo effect—and this is particularly the case because this model assumes that illness has a non-arbitrary medical cause—an assumption which the phenomenon of the nocebo effect contradicts.

25. For a full account of this case see Meador, "Hex Death," 244–45.

Through this contradiction a second world comes into being, which is the inverse of the first. In this world, which the account of Vanders exemplifies, illness has an arbitrary cause, and non-arbitrary treatments (i.e., treatment which is established as non-arbitrary because it out performed placebos) are inefficacious when battling this arbitrary illness. In this world, it is only a type of arbitrary treatment—a placebo—which is able to cure this arbitrary illness—and in this example we observe the placebo outperforming the standard treatment.

Let us now, for the sake of attempting to clarify (or complicate) our concepts of arbitrary and non-arbitrary, imagine an epidemic of such particular cases as the one described in the account of Vanders. Let us imagine hundreds of pugnacious exchanges between voodoo priests and their associates, such that hundreds of hospital beds are filled with individuals who are in a similar situation as Vanders; in which similar types of placebo treatments have to be performed after standard medical treatment fails to yield results. At such a point, given inductive reasoning (as well as the problems which Hume points out concerning inductive reasoning) and the habits that are being formed when treating this disease, it becomes unclear why this particular treatment should be characterized as a placebo. This is the case regardless of how bizarre or artful the treatment is. In a like manner it equally becomes unclear why this particular illness should be understood as arbitrary in nature. Rather, given the imagined scenario of greater frequency of this type of situation, there would appear to be a cause and effect relationship, between the particular treatment curing the disease—and in this relationship, an indistinguishability between the arbitrary and the non-arbitrary nature of it emerges.

Redefining the Placebo Effect and the Possibility That the Placebo Effect Is Getting Stronger

We are somewhat uncertain how the placebo effect was discovered, Shapiro and Shapiro provide early examples of when ideas resembling the placebo effect were first mentioned—which go back to Bishop Berkeley—but this is not the same as discovering a detailed philosophical account concerning why an individual that observes such a phenomenon should label it as something amounting to the placebo effect as opposed to a labelling it something contrary which would connote an effect which is non-arbitrary. Whatever the case may be, it appears that two conditions would be necessary for an idea like the placebo effect to be conceivable. The first condition would be that individuals would need to hold that certain beliefs systems concerning ontology were true while other ones were false. The second condition would be that the individual would hold that although certain belief systems concerning ontology are false, others who falsely believe in them can still experience effects of belief systems—effects which make the belief system appear true. An example of such conditions would be an individual not believing in the gods nor that the gods can heal a person of a fatal illness, but then observing a sick person who has a fatal illness praying to the gods and then being healed. Instead of believing in the gods and that the gods healed the sick person, this non-believing individual might instead offer up an explanation akin to the placebo effect—which in reality is not really an explanation at all, but rather merely a contradictory belief to the one which the formerly sick person holds.

Once the idea of the placebo effect is understood, another idea or belief is necessary for an individual's understanding of the placebo effect to acquire limits or boundaries. This idea is that what causes things with non-arbitrary natures to have non-arbitrary natures cannot be the placebo effect, itself. So, for example, let us again take the case of the sick person who has the fatal disease, who is cured when praying to the gods. The individual who is skeptical of the existence of the gods may conclude that the placebo effect somehow changed the nature of a fatal disease into something not fatal, but this individual does not assume that the nature of the fatal disease itself was produced through an effect like the placebo effect (such as the nocebo effect). If, however, we posit for a moment that there is an indistinguishability between the arbitrary and non-arbitrary nature of things, might we not reconsider how we understand the nature of the placebo effect? For example, if we suppose for a moment that the nature of things is ultimately arbitrary, all former understandings of the placebo effect make no sense. In such a world as described, the placebo effect, as we understand it would not exist. The phenomenon which we would have labelled the placebo effect (in a world where things were non-arbitrary) might better be understood in a world in which the nature of things is arbitrary as "the effect which makes the nature of a things appear permanent, consistent, and dependable, but which can change when confronted with a greater opposite effect." If we assert that there is an indistinguishability between the arbitrary and non-arbitrary nature of things, we might wonder if this alternative understanding of the placebo effect is equally viable.

In recent years it has been suggested that the placebo effect is getting stronger,[26] and although this claim will require further research on the part of scientists in the future—meaning for now it is too soon to establish the validity of such a conclusion—such a phenomenon, it would appear, if true, has the possibility to contribute credence to the position of epistemological agnosticism. Our position would be supported further, if placebos begin to perform as effectively as the drugs being tested in test trials with greater and greater frequency. Newer drugs which are thought to be more effective and powerful, when treating illnesses, should outperform placebos by an even greater margin, but when placebos perform at the same level it suggests an increase in the effectiveness of the placebo effect. For now, it remains unclear (conceptually) if the placebo effect has limits and if so, what those limits are, but we are of the opinion that the phenomenon of the placebo effect—particularly when taken together with the nocebo effect add credence to the idea that there is an indistinguishability between the arbitrary nature and non-arbitrary nature of things.

A Brief Coda on the Construction of Worlds

We have argued for the epistemological position that there is an indistinguishability between the arbitrary and the non-arbitrary nature of things. Given our presentation of the two contemporary phenomena which we suggest add credence to this view, we aimed to show that epistemological agnosticism toward the arbitrary nature of things is a reasonable philosophical position to take. We argued that this position has its origins in Hegel's *Phenomenology of the Spirit* once the three skeptical discoveries are realized. These skeptical discoveries are (1) That what is universal is compatible with what is arbitrary. (2) That coherence epistemologies have the potential to facilitate topsy-turvy worlds that are inverses of each other. (3) That the Spirit which is thought divine is indistinguishable from either a Volksgeist, or the Spirit which Hegel offers, i.e., the divine and human Spirit are unable to be distinguished from each other.

This epistemological situation is one we find to be quite fascinating not because of the uncertainty which it brings per se, but because of the seemingly unlimited creativity this uncertainty leaves room for. Voegelin accuses Hegel of providing his readers with imaginative history,

---

26. For a more comprehensive consideration of this idea refer to chapter 1 of Bauregard, *Brain Wars*, "The Power of Belief to Cure or Kill."

but no history is void of imagination. Geurts utilizes the concept of sensoriums and Bourdieu's notion of history becoming nature to show that any aspect of a nature that humans experience is experienced through a history which shapes the present experience that was the future just moments ago. This process involves imagination. Our agnosticism questions whether such a process of bringing the future into being has any limitations besides the imaginations of human beings.

Appendix A

Some Reflection on the Meaning of "Nature"

THROUGHOUT THIS BOOK THE term "nature" has been defined in a nebulous fashion at best. This is partly because we hoped to demonstrate cogency for the position that there is an indistinguishability between the arbitrary and non-arbitrary nature of things, but it is also partly due to two words which the term "nature" is often contrasted with. The concept of nature is often couched between two other terms, which can serve to contrast it, delineate it, and even (in certain cases) explain its existence. These terms are "supernatural" and "nurture." Let us begin by contrasting the idea of "nature" with the idea of "nurture"—and for this contrast, let us restrict ourselves to a paradigm of naturalism, so that any thoughts of the supernatural will not complicate our contrast. What, then, let us ask, is meant by "nurture" as opposed to "nature" in a naturalistic paradigm? It appears, ostensibly, that nurture is that which can effect change in an object or thing in a variety of ways, but that which remains unaffected by this change is what we might designate to be the nature of a thing. The question then becomes does the influence of what we term "nurture" have any true limits—or are the limits, which we currently observe with respect to nurture merely circumstantial and contingent on our understanding of the universe which is far from complete? Let us refer to a concept of nurture which is capable of enacting limitless effect as "supernurtural." (And let me take a moment to lament that this word did not pervade humanity's vocabulary with the same frequency and tenacity as the word "supernatural" has. For if the concept of supernurtural was as prevalent of a concept as the concept of the supernatural, there

APPENDIX A: SOME REFLECTION ON THE MEANING OF "NATURE"

would have been no need for this book to be written—for every conceptual assertion within these pages would be old hat.)

Let us now contrast the concept of "nature" with the concept of "supernatural." Let us take a rather simple example of a magician turning a dog into a cat simply by uttering a few magic words. We might rightly label this event "supernatural"—but what precisely would we mean by this utterance? We might mean that what we just observed violated our understanding of the laws of nature, and is therefore, best understood as supernatural. We might also state that it is our belief that the nature of a dog is such that it cannot spontaneously become a cat when a magician utters a few magic words. This we find is all that is meant by the term "nature" in this book, if we contrast it with the idea of the supernatural.

But what is meant by "nature" overall is still less clear than this—and here is what I mean: Let us again imagine a dog being spontaneously changed into a cat, but this time it is not a magician uttering magic words. Instead, it is a behavioral scientist uttering words which possess a supernurtural effect, which the dog has been conditioned upon hearing to turn into a cat. With this latter example we would label this effect "supernurtural" as opposed to "supernatural." But now let us imagine that supernurtural effects are ubiquitous, so much so, that they are the norm and not the exception. What then might we mean when we use the term "nature"? I am not entirely sure what we would mean by it, except that if we used it in the former context (i.e., the context in which the supernurtural was not ubiquitous) when in the imagined context that whatever was understood by the word "nature" would carry the connotation that the nature of the thing being referred to was ultimately understood to be arbitrary.

Bibliography

Abadi, Richard V., and Jonathan S. Murphy. "Phenomenology of the Sound-Induced Flash Illusion." *Experimental Brain Research Springer Journal* 232 (2014) 2207–20.
Beauregard, Mario. *Brain Wars: The Scientific Battle over the Existence of the Mind and the Proof That Will Change the Way We Live Our Lives.* New York: HarperOne, 2012.
Cannon, W. B. "Voodoo Death." *American Anthropologist* 44.2 (1942) 169–81.
deVires, Willem. "Hegel's Logic and Philosophy of Mind." In *The Age of German Idealism*, edited by Robert Solomon and Kathleen Higgins, 216–53. Routledge History of Philosophy Volume 6. Routledge: New York, 1993.
Farneth, Molly. *Hegel's Social Ethics: Religion, Conflict, and Rituals of Reconciliation.* Princeton: Princeton University Press, 2017.
Flay, Joseph C. "Hegel's 'Inverted World.'" *The Review of Metaphysics* 23.4 (1970) 662–78.
Forster, Michael N. *Hegel's Idea of a Phenomenology of Spirit.* Chicago: University of Chicago Press, 1998.
Gadamer, Hans-Georg. *Hegel's Dialectic: Five Hermeneutical Studies.* New Haven: Yale University Press, 1976.
Geurts, Kathryn Linn. *Culture and the Senses: Bodily Ways of Knowing in an African Community.* Berkeley: University of California Press, 2002.
Hahn, Robert A. "The Nocebo Phenomenon: Scope and Foundations." In *The Placebo Effect: An Interdisciplinary Exploration*, edited by Anne Harrington, 56–76. Cambridge: Harvard University Press, 1997.
Hegel, G. W. F. *Faith and Knowledge.* Translated by Walter Cerf and H. S. Harris. Albany: State University of New York Press, 1977.
———. *Phenomenology of Spirit.* Oxford: Oxford University Press, 1977.
Hyppolite, Jean. *Genesis and Structure of Hegel's "Phenomenology of Spirit."* Evanston, IL: Northwestern University Press, 1974.
Inwood, Michael. *A Hegel Dictionary: The Blackwell Philosopher Dictionaries.* Oxford: Blackwell, 1992.
———. "Solomon, Hegel, and Truth." *The Review of Metaphysics* 31.2 (1977) 272–82.
Lauer, Quentin. *A Reading of Hegel's "Phenomenology of Spirit."* New York: Fordham University Press, 1976.
Loewenberg, Jacob. *Hegel's Phenomenology: Dialogues on the Life of Mind.* La Salle, IL: Open Court, 1965.

BIBLIOGRAPHY

MacIntyre, Alasdair. "Hegel on Faces and Skulls." In *Hegel: A Collection of Critical Essays*, edited by Alasdair MacIntyre, 219–36. Garden City, NY: Anchor, 1972.

Magee, Glenn Alexander. *Hegel and the Hermetic Tradition*. Ithaca, NY: Cornell University Press, 2001.

Mandel, Oscar. Introduction to *The Land of Upside Down*, by Ludwig Tieck, 7–26. Cranbury, NJ: Associated University Presses, 1978.

Meador, Clifton K. "Hex Death: Voodoo Magic or Persuasion?" *Southern Medical Journal* 85.3 (1992) 244–47.

Olsson, Erick J. "Coherentism." In *The Routledge Companion to Epistemology*, edited by Sven Bernecker and Duncan Pritchard, 257–67. New York: Routledge, 2014.

Pals, Danel. *Nine Theories of Religion*. 3rd ed. Oxford: Oxford University Press, 2006.

Quine, W. V. "Two Dogmas of Empiricism." *The Philosophical Review* 60.1 (1951) 20–43.

Quine, W. V., and J. S. Ullian. *Web of Belief*. New York: Random House, 1978.

Sedgwick, Sally. *Hegel's Critique of Kant: From Dichotomy to Identity*. Oxford: Oxford University Press, 2012.

Shams, Ladan, et al. "Visual Illusion Induced by Sound." *Cognitive Brain Research* 14 (2002) 147–52.

Shapiro, Arthur K., and Elaine Shapiro. *The Powerful Placebo: From Ancient Priest to Modern Physician*. Baltimore: John Hopkins University Press, 1997.

Solomon, Robert. *From Hegel to Existentialism*. Oxford: Oxford University Press, 1987.

———. "Hegel's Epistemology." *American Philosophical Quarterly* 11.4 (1974) 277–89.

———. "Hegel's *Phenomenology of Spirit*." In *The Age of German Idealism*, edited by Robert Solomon and Kathleen Higgins, 181–215. Routledge History of Philosophy Volume 6. New York: Routledge, 1993.

———. *In the Spirit of Hegel*. Oxford: Oxford University Press, 1983.

———. "Truth and Self-Satisfaction." *The Review of Metaphysics* 28.4 (1975) 698–724.

Stern, Robert. *Hegelian Metaphysics*. Oxford: Oxford University Press, 2009.

Van Inwagen, Peter. *An Essay on Free Will*. Oxford: Clarendon, 1983.

Verene, Donald Phillip. *Hegel's Recollection: A Study of Images in the "Phenomenology of Spirit."* Albany: State University of New York Press, 1985.

Voegelin, Eric. "On Hegel—A Study in Sorcery." In *The Study of Time*, edited by J. T. Fraser et al., 418–51. New York: Springer-Verlag, 1972.

Winfield, Richard Dien. *Hegel's "Phenomenology of Spirit": A Critical Rethinking in Seventeen Lectures*. Lanham, MD: Rowman & Littlefield, 2013.

———. "Hegel versus the New Orthodoxy." In *Hegel & His Critics: Philosophy in the Aftermath of Hegel*, edited by William Desmond, 219–40. New York: State University of New York Press, 1989.

www.ingramcontent.com/pod-product-compliance
Lightning Source LLC
Chambersburg PA
CBHW050819160426
43192CB00010B/1815